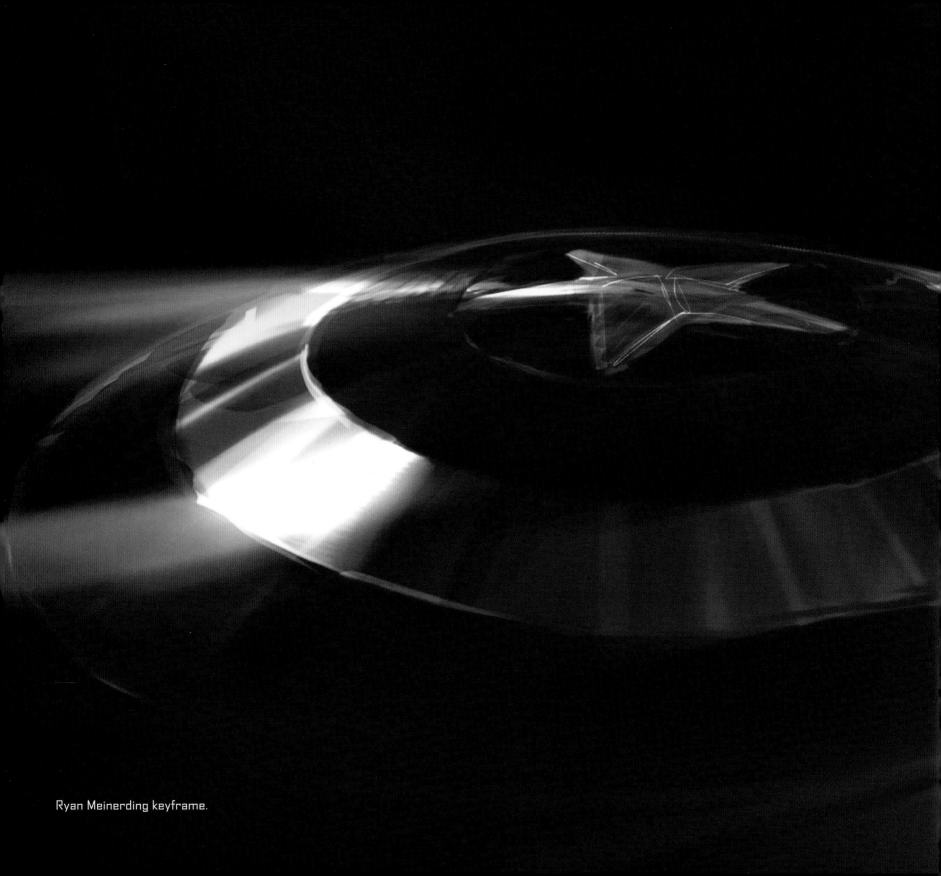

Ryan Meinerding keyframe.

MARVEL STUDIOS

THE INFINITY SAGA

THE ART OF

MARVEL STUDIOS

CAPTAIN AMERICA
THE WINTER SOLDIER

WRITTEN BY
MARIE JAVINS

FOREWORD BY
ANTHONY & JOE RUSSO

AFTERWORD BY
RYAN MEINERDING

BOOK DESIGN BY
JEFF POWELL

CAPTAIN AMERICA CREATED BY
JOE SIMON & JACK KIRBY

TITAN BOOKS

FOR MARVEL PUBLISHING
JEFF YOUNGQUIST, Editor
SARAH SINGER, Editor, Special Projects
JEREMY WEST, Manager, Licensed Publishing
SVEN LARSEN, VP, Licensed Publishing
DAVID GABRIEL, SVP Print, Sales & Marketing
C.B. CEBULSKI, Editor in Chief

FOR MARVEL STUDIOS 2014
KEVIN FEIGE, President
LOUIS D'ESPOSITO, Co-President
VICTORIA ALONSO, Executive Vice President,
    Visual Effects
NATE MOORE, Senior Vice President, Production
    & Development
WILL CORONA PILGRIM, Creative Manager,
    Research & Development
TRINH TRAN, Creative Executive
RYAN POTTER, Principal Counsel
ERIKA DENTON, Clearances Director
RANDY McGOWAN, VP Technical Operations
ALEXEI KRASSOVSKY, Digital Asset Coordinator
MITCH BELL, Vice President, Physical Production
ALEXIS AUDITORE, Physical Assets Coordinator

MARVEL STUDIOS: THE INFINITY SAGA - CAPTAIN AMERICA:
THE WINTER SOLDIER: THE ART OF THE MOVIE

ISBN: 9781803365602
E-BOOK ISBN: 9781803365886

First edition: October 2024

10 9 8 7 6 5 4 3 2 1

Published by Titan Books
A division of Titan Publishing Group Ltd
144 Southwark St, London SE1 0UP

www.titanbooks.com

Did you enjoy this book? We love to hear from our readers. Please e-mail us at: readerfeedback@titanmail.com or write to Reader Feedback at the above address.

To receive advance information, news, competitions, and
exclusive offers online, please sign up for the Titan
newsletter on our website: www.titanbooks.com

A CIP catalogue record for this title is available from the
British Library.

Printed in China

Rodney Fuentebella keyframe.

Rodney Fuentebella keyframe.

CONTENTS

I t was in the late '70s, sitting in front of a Zenith television in the living room of the duplex we were raised in, that we watched The *French Connection* for the first time. It was on the late show. Maybe it was a Saturday night. Our father enjoyed movies as a way to decompress from the work week. He had a high motor and was a bit of an insomniac—two conditions we inherited from him—so he loved the late show as a way to occupy his restless night hours. Most weekends, he'd let us stay up to watch movies with him—so that he could share his love of cinema with us, and so that he had some company to laugh with him at the Bowery Boys. Or root for Bogart. Or be amused and vaguely frightened at any number of Hammer films.

But it was our viewing of *The French Connection* that evening that had a lasting impact on us. The emotions we felt when we watched it. The visceral intensity. Both filmmakers and audiences are well aware of the brilliance of the car chase in that film. But Friedkin made a walking foot chase equally as exciting to us. Our young minds had never seen action so expertly executed. The camera work. The emotional commitment of the actors. The sound design. The juxtaposition of images. The escalation of stakes. Thirty-five years later, there are moments we can still recall from our first viewing of that film. That's impactful filmmaking.

The definition of action films may have been slightly misappropriated by splashy, expensive movies from the late '80s. All movies expertly made, and movies we loved—*Die Hard, Predator, First Blood*—but the term has a more universal meaning than the narrow genre application it's fallen into. As Webster points out, action is "the fact or process of doing something, typically to achieve aim." The most significant part of the definition for our process as filmmakers—and what we learned from Friedkin that night in our living room—is that, as stated, action has the typical intent of achieving aim. For us, aim is a goal. Aim is storytelling. Aim is narrative.

In all of our favorite action sequences, the character has an emotional aim. Personal stakes. The aim can be selfish or vaguely corrupt, as it is in *The French Connection*, but it's an aim nonetheless. And that aim is the engine of the action. It's the engine of every beat of the action. Each beat in a great action sequence is an inventive, detailed, harrowing, and thoughtful mini-narrative about whether the character will achieve their said aim by the end of the sequence—and, ultimately, by the end of the film.

In *The French Connection*'s car chase, Popeye Doyle wants to capture a hitman who just tried to kill him. The aim on a plot level is clear and simple. Yet on a narrative level, it's much more complex: Doyle is a restless, overzealous cop who is greatly disliked by a federal agent named Mulderig, who blames Doyle's recklessness for the death of a fellow policeman. In capturing this hitman—and seizing a massive shipment of heroin heading for New York City— Doyle has the unspoken aim of vindicating himself as a great cop whose current achievement will outshine his marred history. What made the car chase so groundbreaking was Doyle's desperate commitment to his aim. This desperation was infused into every microfiber of every action beat in the movie. And that's what made it such a seminal film.

It was in 1982 that we saw *Blow Out* for the first time. On a VHS tape rented from a small video store nestled between a 7-Eleven and a Mr. Hero in the eastern suburbs of Cleveland. And even though De Palma is often thought of as a master of tension, by Webster's definition, he's also quite possibly one of the best action directors of the 20th century. His characters' aims are specific and rootable (even though they tragically don't often achieve them). And his true gift as a filmmaker, like Friedkin, is the ability to create protracted sequences where the character's aim is constantly in danger of being thwarted. Long sequences filled with inventive, detailed, harrowing, and thoughtful mini-narratives. The climax in *Blow Out*. The stairwell scene in *The Untouchables*. The white-vault scene in *Mission: Impossible*.

It's from Friedkin and De Palma that we drew a lot of our inspiration for *Captain America: The Winter Soldier*. We tried to give the characters clear aims—most often survival or escape, and then attempted to complicate those aims through narrative. Nick Fury's hubris makes him vulnerable. Steve Rogers' disenfranchisement keeps him off balance. We then tried to follow Friedkin and De Palma's example by creating long sequences filled with mini-narratives where the characters' aims are constantly in danger of being thwarted. The sequence where Fury is ambushed in his car, and then pursued as he attempts to escape, ultimately undone by the Winter Soldier. The sequence where Cap is attacked in the elevator. Or where Winter Soldier assaults Cap, Natasha, and Sam on the freeway, and Steve is forced to battle him for the first time to save Natasha's life.

The effort to keep these long sequences detailed and inventive was both arduous and fulfilling. And required an incredible amount of collaboration. As did every detail of the film.

From the writers, Christopher Markus and Steven McFeeley, who spent more than two years expertly fashioning the screenplay.

To our Producer, the brilliant auteur of the MCU, Kevin Feige.

To our Executive Producers, Lou D'Esposito and Victoria Alonso, the best in the business at what they do—and, more importantly, two of the best people we know.

To our Co-Producer Nate Moore, who functioned as the third Russo Brother on this film, and whose exceptional taste and creativity is expressed in the movie as much as ours.

To our Cinematographer Trent Oplach, whose visceral and dynamic camera work and trenchant lighting brought the script to life.

To Peter Wenham, our production designer, whose beautiful, sleek designs enriched the narrative and grounded the storytelling.

To Dan DeLeeuw, our Visual Effects Supervisor, whose intelligence, artistry, tenacity, and encyclopedic knowledge helped sculpt 2,400 special effects shots into works of art.

To Ryan Meinerding, whose staggering conceptual art—which you are most likely familiar with if you're a fan of the Marvel Cinematic Universe—has helped define much of the look of the MCU to this point.

To Judianna Makovsky, whose meticulous attention to detail and fidelity to construction made for brilliantly faithful cinematic interpretations of our heroes' costumes.

To Russell Bobbitt, THE prop master in the film business.

To our storyboard artists—Darrin Denlinger, Richard Bennett, and Federico D'Alessandro, our brothers in arms—whose gifted visual storytelling and ingenious ideas were the soul of our action sequences.

And the list goes on and on.

Another misappropriation in the film business is that the director is a singular, all-powerful force behind the creation of a film. It's a convenient media-inspired myth, where an elaborate and inscrutable process of collaboration becomes reduced down to a single name and face. Admittedly, this concept may be accurate for certain directors that are gifted in a wide array of specialized areas—those who meticulously storyboard their own films, design sets or costumes, orchestrate their own scores, operate their own cameras, light their own sets, edit their own films, etc. For us, as brothers, who've worked closely together on a daily basis for the last fifteen years, it's a highly collaborative art. Our job as filmmakers is to effectively manage a collection of incredibly talented individuals and fashion their work into a cohesive vision. Contained in this book is the work of some of the amazingly gifted individuals we had the opportunity to do that with on this film. Hope you enjoy it as we have...

Anthony & Joe Russo
Anthony & Joe Russo
2014

CAPTAIN STEVE ROGERS: AGENT OF S.H.I.E.L.D.

Steve Rogers is a man out of time, a kid from New York City who no longer recognizes the home he left in *Captain America: The First Avenger*. A man who fell into suspended animation seventy years ago, when the Allies were fighting fascism in Europe, and woke up in the modern world—having missed a divided Berlin, the Beatles, the Civil Rights movement, men on the moon, Watergate, and *Star Wars*.

"Captain America is soul-searching to see who he. Is he happy to be back on the job? The world has changed. Where does he fit in?" Executive Producer and EVP of VFX and Post-Production Victoria Alonso explains.

Among the collection of geniuses, spies, and demi-gods known as the Avengers, old-fashioned soldier Steve Rogers seemed the normal one. But after the disparate group of heroes rallied to fight off an alien invasion in *Marvel's The Avengers*, they disbanded and scattered, going back to the lives they'd been leading before Thor's brother Loki set his eyes on the otherworldly Tesseract and used it to open a portal into another galaxy.

Tony Stark returned to Malibu to build more Iron Man armors and wrestle his inner demons after throwing a nuclear bomb into outer space turned his world upside-down, while Thor moved on to battlefronts in other dimensions. Dr. Bruce Banner—aka Hulk—melted back into anonymity and his wandering ways. Black Widow and Hawkeye kept up their espionage work for S.H.I.E.L.D.

Meanwhile, Captain America stayed with the only authority he knew. A year after the events of *Marvel's The Avengers*, Steve Rogers is working for S.H.I.E.L.D. Director Nick Fury in Washington, D.C.

"Cap stays with S.H.I.E.L.D. in the new era in which he's found himself because he can't go back in time and live in the '40s again," Producer Kevin Feige says. "But he's not necessarily comfortable there."

Captain America throws himself into his work with S.H.I.E.L.D. with the single-minded focus of a soldier—or anyone avoiding some hard questions about the future.

"He just busies himself by going on mission after mission," Co-Producer Nate Moore says. "Because he's been doing that, he hasn't completely adjusted to the modern world—meaning he doesn't have a lot of friends outside of work, and he doesn't really know what to do with his free time."

Eventually, Steve begins to realize his loyalty to S.H.I.E.L.D.

Captain America, Agent 13, Nick Fury and the agents of S.H.I.E.L.D.— from the cover to *Captain America (2005) #9* by Steve Epting with colors by Frank D'Armata.

The Triskelion, from *The Ultimates 2 (2005) #1*—penciled by Bryan Hitch, inked by Paul Neary and colored by Laura Martin.

might be misplaced. Captain America is a soldier, not a spy. He fights for freedom. But as he learns more about the nuanced world in which Nick Fury and Black Widow operate, he begins to realize that his definition of freedom was formed in simpler times, when evil had a clear face.

"You're plucking a guy out of the Greatest Generation and slamming him into this cultural mess that we're in now," Director Joe Russo explains.

Director Anthony Russo continues: "All he knew was Allies versus Nazis. Cap's such a great character because, unlike us, Cap hasn't been led incrementally through the years. He's a great person to react to because he hasn't been corrupted or half-compromised in any way."

Nick Fury, however, is no stranger to moral compromise. He does whatever it takes to get the job done, but always in the name of the greater good. But S.H.I.E.L.D.'s latest preemptive endeavor—Project Insight—has increased surveillance of innocents around the world via three new Helicarriers and a network of targeting satellites, and Steve Rogers begins to suspect the agency he works for has overstepped its bounds. As Tony Stark pointed out in *Marvel's The Avengers*, Nick Fury isn't just a spy. "He is *the* spy. His secrets have secrets."

S.H.I.E.L.D.'s methods infringe on the very freedoms for which Captain America stands. But it isn't until Fury is targeted for assassination that Captain America realizes that S.H.I.E.L.D. has been compromised at its very heart. What had been a complex network of moral ambiguity is now clearly tainted with corruption. Captain America fights for freedom, but how can he fight an enemy he can't even identify? His moral conundrum tangles him within a web of intrigue and deceit; alongside Black Widow, the sentinel of liberty becomes a fugitive in a world of conspiracy.

"Our first Captain America film was a World War II picture," Feige says. "In this one, we tip our hat to the political thrillers of the '70s like *Three Days of the Condor, The Parallax View* and *All the President's Men*—but it's also a contemporary action film."

Marvel's recent *Captain America* comic books had already set a precedent for an espionage thriller.

"The Ed Brubaker/Steve Epting run is definitely a huge inspiration for this film," Moore says. "It was an amazing run."

Writer Ed Brubaker was already known for his crime-fiction comic-book work before he began writing super-hero comics. He relaunched *Captain America* with artist Steve Epting in 2004 and stayed on the series for eight years.

"I was trying to do something that felt like a tense international political thriller—but with A.I.M., Hydra, Captain America, and S.H.I.E.L.D. instead of the FBI and terrorists," Brubaker says. "I wanted to put that tone into the Marvel Universe, sort of like what Steranko did with Nick Fury and Captain America back in the '60s."

Writer/artist Jim Steranko had been instrumental in the 1960s evolution of Marvel's comic-book style. Most notably in the pages of *Nick Fury, Agent of S.H.I.E.L.D.* and *Captain America*, Steranko introduced innovative design and thrilling spy stories to the medium at a time when Steve Rogers had been brought back into the active world of Marvel heroes. The modern version of Captain America had only been around for five years when Brubaker first became aware of the character.

"I first heard of Captain America and Bucky when I was three years old and my family lived on the Navy base in Gitmo. They showed those Marvel cartoons from the late '60s then on the Navy base's TV channel. The first one I ever saw was the origin of Captain America where Bucky stumbles into the tent and finds out his friend is Captain America and decides to be his partner, but I always knew the story of how Bucky got blown up by Baron Zemo at the end of the war," Brubaker explains.

When Brubaker's family moved to San Diego five years later, he went to his first comic-book convention to search for the back issue in which teen-sidekick James "Bucky" Barnes had been blown up.

There was no such back issue. Marvel Editor in Chief Stan Lee had decided to bring back Captain America in 1964 as a modern Rip Van Winkle, but he'd added a timeless level of tragedy to Steve Rogers' story. Joe Simon and Jack Kirby's 1941 Captain America would not work in the '60s as a patriot fighting Nazis. But he worked brilliantly as a man out of time, his quest for freedom and justice contrasting with the complex political atmosphere of the era.

Bucky had been left in the past, retroactively written out of the story—his dying breath the last thing Captain America saw before being frozen in ice. Twenty-three years earlier, Lee's first Marvel work had been a two-page prose story featuring Bucky, but teen sidekicks were simply no longer needed.

Lee explains Captain America's resurrection: "When he wakes up, he feels like an anachronism. He couldn't understand Woodstock, and he couldn't understand what was going on with the hippies and with drugs and so forth. And he had trouble fitting into the civilization that he found himself in. And then we had the usual villains and fights. But by giving him a little more personality and some problems to cope with of his own of adjusting to the world that he found, somehow the readers identified with him, and he became one of the most popular characters."

Steve Rogers—the once and future Captain America—from *Steve Rogers: Super-Soldier (2010) #1*, by Dale Eaglesham with colors by Andy Troy.

The Marvel Cinematic Universe works on a different timeline than the comic books. In the movies, Captain America has only been awake a short time.

"We embrace the conflict that Steve Rogers has had in the comics from the moment he thawed out," Kevin Feige says. Captain America's resurrection in the modern era is not the same as him having to make sense of the JFK assassination and Watergate, but *Captain America: The Winter Soldier* embraces the tone of the older comics.

Bucky stayed dead in the Marvel Universe for decades, but Brubaker had imagined bringing him back to life since he was eight years old. He finally got that chance in 2005, when *Captain America* Editor Tom Brevoort gave Brubaker and artist Steve Epting the go-ahead to resurrect Bucky as the lethal assassin Winter Soldier.

"We wanted to develop Winter Soldier in a way that would be respectful of the Stan and Jack years of *Captain America*, making sure that the story we were telling fit with the continuity of those stories," Brubaker says. "We replaced the tragedy of Steve Rogers'

best friend getting blown up with one that was even worse: the tragedy of him becoming something they'd both despise, which is an enemy of your own country."

Steve Epting had drawn *Captain America* hundreds of times as the artist on a popular three-year run of *Avengers* a decade earlier, but now his job was to create a modern version of a boy-hero from the 1940s.

"We went into the design of Winter Soldier with some specific requirements." Epting says. "The first was the metal arm that, as part of Ed's storyline, would replace the one Bucky lost during his last mission in World War II, and the second was the domino mask. We wanted some visual links to his Bucky costume, and the domino mask was the most obvious."

Epting added rows of snaps to recall Bucky's original double-breasted shirt and a red star to tie him to the Russians, who had fished the frozen hero out of the sea before indoctrinating and training the amnesiac Bucky as an assassin. He'd been kept in cryogenic stasis between missions and had aged only a few years during the intervening decades, making it difficult to update the character in a way that Steve Rogers would not recognize his former partner. Epting initially tried giving Winter Soldier a haircut similar to Bucky's.

"Ed, Tom Brevoort, Editor in Chief Joe Quesada, and I all agreed early on that the character did not look tough enough at that point. My recollection is that Joe suggested the longer hair—which did make him look more formidable, if not a bit sinister, and along with the mask helped obscure his face enough so that Captain America could not be sure it was really Bucky until he got face-to-face with him."

Both in the comics and on-screen, Captain America finds himself hindered in battle once he recognizes the Winter Soldier—unable to give his all while fighting his best friend.

"Bucky was a wonderful guy—his best friend—and Steve thought he died and felt some guilt for his death," says Stephen McFeely, co-writer of the film along with Christopher Markus. "Then he finds out Bucky is actually alive, trying to kill him and working for the bad guys. There is no worse thing that could happen to Steve Rogers, particularly in a movie that's about trust."

His former sidekick is highly skilled and powerful, and Steve Rogers is handicapped by sentimentality—and by the gut instinct that Bucky cannot possibly be in control of his faculties.

"Captain America is still a man out of time in the movie, but the other important aspect of this film is friendship," Creative Executive Trinh Tran says. "He thought he lost his friend in WWII, and now he realizes at this movie's midway point that his friend is back and working on the other side."

Steve Rogers develops new friendships during the course of the film. Black Widow has fled with him, helping him hide in the shadows, and Sam Wilson is introduced as Captain America's best friend and partner in the modern era. Steve and Natasha initially go to Sam for shelter because he is outside the S.H.I.E.L.D. system

The Falcon, from the cover to *Ultimate Nightmare (2004) #4*, by Steve Epting with colors by Frank D'Armata.

Clockwise from top left: Nick Fury (Bryan Hitch), Black Widow (Tomm Coker & Daniel Freedman), Sharon Carter and Maria Hill (Mike Perkins & Frank D'Armata), Jack Rollins (Paul Neary, Kim DeMulder & Bernie Jaye), Alexander Pierce (Stefano Caselli & Sunny Gho), and Batroc the Leaper

Ryan Meinerding, Head of Visual Development, talks about the conflict between Falcon's original 1969 comic-book persona and his appearance on-screen: "You don't get to a place of modernization with Falcon. I feel like his fans love the red-and-white costume and the pet falcon, which he doesn't have here."

On-screen, Wilson trades his spandex and red feathers for the Exo-7 Falcon apparatus and doesn't have a mental connection to birds. He isn't the only supporting character with changes for the cinematic world: Brock Rumlow and Georges Batroc show up in the Marvel Cinematic Universe, but in very different ways than they appear on the page.

"We're having fun with some second- and third-tier characters that otherwise wouldn't have a place in our films by using them in ways that still serve a narrative purpose and also give the characters an extra boost," Moore says. "We may not see Crossbones down the line, so why not use that name and that character? Again, that's a nod to publishing in a way that doesn't break the logic of our film, but can still be really fun."

Captain America also briefly meets Agent 13, a S.H.I.E.L.D. operative working for Nick Fury. Is it her job to protect Steve Rogers or to monitor him? Like everything else in which Fury is involved, this area is gray. But while Cap's relationship with Fury is complicated, they are ultimately on the same team.

"Throughout the whole film, he struggles with that relationship with Fury," Tran says. "Steve has a different point of view, and he's always conflicted. But at the end, Steve has accomplished in a way what he wanted. Steve truly becomes Captain America in the modern world."

Steve Rogers may be a man out of time, but his core values are ultimately timeless. His humble characteristics were what made Dr. Erskine choose a ninety-pound asthmatic over powerful soldiers and bullies. The Super-Soldier Serum made the man without more physically powerful, but it did not change the man within. The serum simply amplified the characteristics that Steve already possessed.

Captain America is an icon who believes in transparency and justice, not in S.H.I.E.L.D.'s preemptive strikes or Nick Fury's attempts to save people from themselves at any cost. His values do not evolve to fit the world. But sometimes, the world evolves to fit him. ★

CHAPTER ONE
TROUBLED
WATERS

A ship of secrets has been hijacked on the high seas of the Indian Ocean. S.H.I.E.L.D.'s S.T.R.I.K.E. team parachutes through the night sky to recover the Lemurian Star and its hostages from pirates led by Georges Batroc. Captain America takes point in his stealth costume. Black Widow and agent Brock Rumlow follow in his wake.

The set for the Lemurian Star scene is real, not digital, according to Co-Producer Nate Moore. "Our Production Designer Peter Wenham and our Location Manager James Lin found a ship called the Sea Launch Commander," he explains. "It's docked in Long Beach, and it goes out four or five times a year and launches satellites from the Equator."

"The Lemurian Star was one small component compared with all the rest of the action sequences that we had to resolve," Wenham says. "Getting hold of a container ship is an immensely complicated, difficult, and expensive thing to do. But one of my objectives was to retain and punctuate the movie's scope with a given amount of money."

The scenes were filmed at the dock, facing the horizon line instead of the Port of Long Beach, with visual effects added later.

"Shooting practically lends a different texture to the film," Moore says. "That's a real deck, that's a real railing, that's a real bridge—all that stuff actually exists."

James Carson concept art.

The Lemurian Star itself is no less thrilling than the scene taking place on it. The set actually comprises two vessels—a launch vessel similar to an oil rig, and a more traditional ship.

"Two ships go to each satellite launch," Peter Wenham explains. "After final checks on the satellite, they evacuate the rig and everyone boards the other vessel. They sail several miles away from where the actual satellite is, and then launch."

Concept Artist James Carson was tasked with creating the set's look. "For our Lemurian Star, I essentially integrated the two Sea Launch ships into one," Carson says. "I added detail and structure to help it feel right, keeping it within the Marvel Universe. The Sea Launch is as fantastic as any film concept—maybe better because it actually exists and functions."

Marvel Studios Head of Visual Development Ryan Meinerding was responsible for developing Captain America's stealth look for the Lemurian Star scene. "The Russo brothers wanted to show that Steve is being asked to go places where he wouldn't necessarily go. He's stepping away from the red, white, and blue, and is willing to put on a costume that makes him more battle-ready," Meinerding says. "There are obvious visual connotations for dropping away the patriotism, but it also shows he's willing to do night missions and black ops—things you wouldn't think he'd be willing to do. And he's willing to do that because he believes in the greater good of S.H.I.E.L.D."

Ryan Meinerding concept art.

Meinerding: "I think of it as the super-soldier costume because in the comics it was worn by Steve Rogers when Bucky was Captain America, and he was officially known as Steve Rogers, Super-Soldier. Everyone else kept calling it the stealth costume, but it will always be the super-soldier costume in my mind. The suit from the comics was designed by Marko Djurdjevic, and it is a brillant reimagining of the character."

Ryan Meinerding concept art.

21

"I worked very hard on Cap's stealth helmet," Meinerding says. "I found that it didn't have that many visible corners in *First Avenger* and *The Avengers*, making it almost difficult to tell whether his head was turning. So we spent a lot of time on really getting that helmet as close to his head as possible, so much so that it's actually designed to have a cut line. It hinges open where the wing is. It fit all-in-one around his head in the previous movies, and therefore the helmet ended up a little bit big. So in an effort to get it as tight to Chris's head as possible, we came up with that design solution. And I think he looks the best he's ever looked in that film."

"We spent a great deal of time modeling the helmets and getting them correct to look really good on Chris Evans," says Shane Mahan, Physical Suit Effects Supervisor at Legacy Effects, which created the helmets. "They're really balanced to his face. An awful lot of R&D and sculpting and re-sculpting and casting and testing and photo-testing went into making them look really cool."

Meinerding: "As a longtime Cap fan, the other labor of love I had was to get his ears exposed. That's a Captain America thing to me—his classic look has his ears showing. In terms of getting the helmet close to his head and actually feeling more like Captain America even without the protruding wings, it was important that I try one last time to have his ears exposed."

Andy Park concept art.

24

Concept Artist Andy Park played with different materials for Black Widow's appearance. "I experimented with giving her costume a two-tone look not only in values but also in sheen and material," Park says. "Her past costumes pretty much had her in one consistent material throughout the outfit, with the lines created mostly with tubing and stitch lines. With this take on the classic Black Widow look, I wanted the lines of the costume to be created by the transition from one material to the next."

25

Costume Designer Judianna Markovsky aimed to give Black Widow a functional-yet-alluring look. "Natasha's hair this time is more sleek and simple, and the new lines in her Black Widow suit create a very sexy silhouette," Markovsky says. "I experimented with creating textured fabrics that stretch, but don't look like a printed stretch."

Executive Producer and EVP of VFX and Post-Production Victoria Alonso describes Black Widow's role on the Lemurian Star: "She has a phenomenal scene and keeps up with all those boys. Action is not just for men."

Every time I work for Marvel, I'm challenged to make something cool out of something that just exists in life," Property Master Russell Bobbitt says with a laugh. "For the data drive, I married the S.H.I.E.L.D. world to a normal USB drive."

Black Widow needed to use the data drive quickly, so Bobbitt added a spring-loaded button to pop out handles.

"The retractable handles add a more serious feel to the piece," Concept Illustrator John Eaves says. "Russell wanted

to see the final design in silver as well as a dark metal look. The element of some internal lighting along the sides was added as a final touch."

Getting the data drive to light up as intended required some planning. "I had to coordinate with the Art Department and the Production Designer to make sure that whatever they put in the set would accept a real USB hub," Bobbitt says.

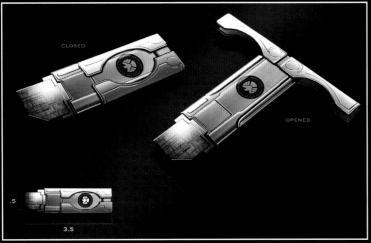

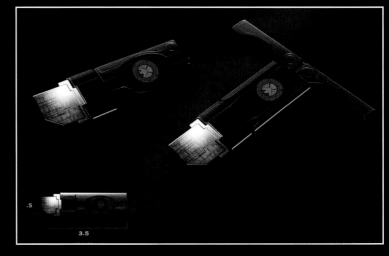

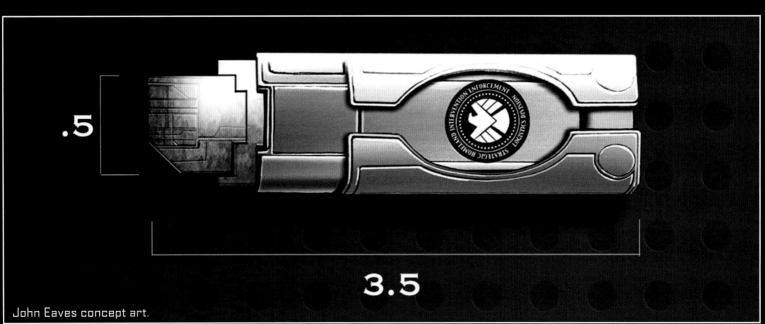

John Eaves concept art.

Black Widow's arsenal also includes her high-tech bracelets, which can produce anything from a Widow's Bite shooting disk to a grappling hook, Bobbitt explains. "We added all these great cut lines to the bracelets so that at any point in the computer-graphic world, we could open up a hatch or slide a little panel that would then reveal anything that the directors choose to in post-production."

Eaves drew several versions with a variety of firing mechanisms. "For a final addition to the bracelet, we added a choker wire," Eaves says. "The first pass featured a wire with a full pull ring. This idea looked good, but practically would take some work to pull over Black Widow's entire hand. So for the final version, we did a partial ring that made deployment easier."

BRACLET FIRING DISC

CHOKER CORD

WIDOW'S DISC

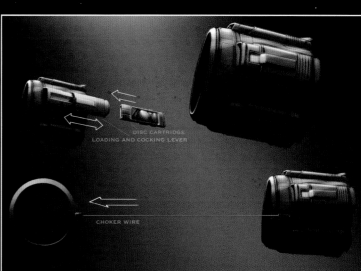

DISC CARTRIDGE
LOADING AND COCKING LEVER

CHOKER WIRE

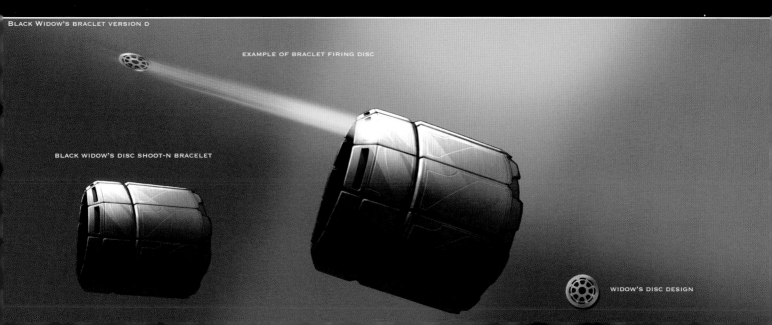

BLACK WIDOW'S BRACLET VERSION D

EXAMPLE OF BRACLET FIRING DISC

BLACK WIDOW'S DISC SHOOT-N BRACELET

WIDOW'S DISC DESIGN

BROCK RUMLOW

Costume Illustrator Christian Cordella, who comes from a family of fashion designers in Italy, worked in collaboration with Costume Designer Judianna Makovsky. Designing Rumlow's S.T.R.I.K.E. suit took him more than four months. "We wanted to create the Marvel SWAT suit, not just something you can buy off the rack," he says. "And so there were different ideas and options to see how many pockets worked best—less pockets, more pockets. Because Rumlow wears parachute gear on top, the concept was to keep it as sleek and functional as possible. After so long, I think I know enough about SWAT suits to be able to do a line of them."

Christian Cordella costume illustration.

Markovsky found developing the fabrics to be the most challenging aspect of creating costumes for *Captain America: The Winter Soldier.* "We wanted something that looked more like real fabric—Kevlar or high-tech nylons. But because of all the action they must have stretch," Markovsky says. "I didn't want to see any printing or stretchiness—just texture. The collaboration with the genius costume cutters, Dale Wibben and Marilyn Madsen, and tailor, Dennis Kim, is what really makes these costumes come to life."

GEORGES BATROC

The pirates' leader is Georges Batroc, but these are not scrappy buccaneers. These modern-day mercenaries are well-funded and armed with top-of-the-line tactical gear.

Costume Illustrator Mariano Diaz describes his take on Batroc: "Judianna Markovsky liked the idea of having him wear a jumper with a zip-up neck, and MMA type gloves. Batroc is a known 'kicker' in the comics, so I added the boots."

Mariano Diaz costume illustration.

Concept Artist Andrew Kim also took a pass at designing Batroc. "I tried to portray a more finessed pirate who's proficient in parkour," Kim says. "His form-fitting costumes were designed to show that he's clean, organized, sleek, and quick."

Andrew Kim concept art.

Rodney Fuentebella concept art.

Seeking to preserve the essence of Batroc's comic-book costume, Markovsky and her team researched real-life pirates. "They wear casual sweaters and track suits. I thought it would be a great way to incorporate the reality of a track suit with the burgundy and gold lines of the comic costume, then add all the combat gear to keep it functional and based in reality."

35

LEMURIAN STAR RESCUE
Storyboards BY Darrin Denlinger

"The directors wanted Cap to have a new, efficient, and smooth fighting technique, so we studied footage of Krav Maga fighters and parkour athletes," Storyboard Artist Darrin Denlinger says. "My only mandate here was to get Cap from point A to point B in the coolest way possible, and I had an enormous playground in which to play. Through it all, I collaborated with the genius Animatics Editor Coral D'Alessandro to hone and massage the sequence."

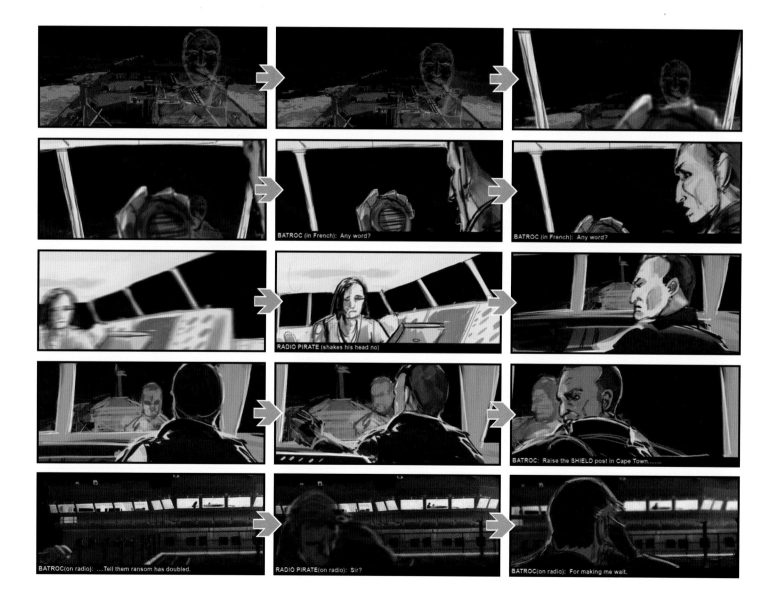

Coral D'Alessandro explains her work: "I cut together storyboards with music and sound effects, working closely with the artists to combine everything into a final product that mimics the experience of watching the finished film. My focus here was doing justice to Darrin's stellar work by heightening the emotions and tempo in the scene. I used a mix of quick cuts for increasing energy and tension along with chaotic sound effects and a soundtrack that tied everything together into an exciting sequence."

Denlinger: "In my opinion, the animatic is the absolute best way to present a storyboard sequence. It allows me control over timing, character blocking, and choreography that is just not possible when pitching sequences on stacks of three-panel paper. When Coral does her magic with sound effects and music, the end result is a much more accurate and exciting vision of how a sequence could appear on screen.

"One of the beautiful things about working for Marvel is that they truly embrace storyboard artists, particularly to create animatics."

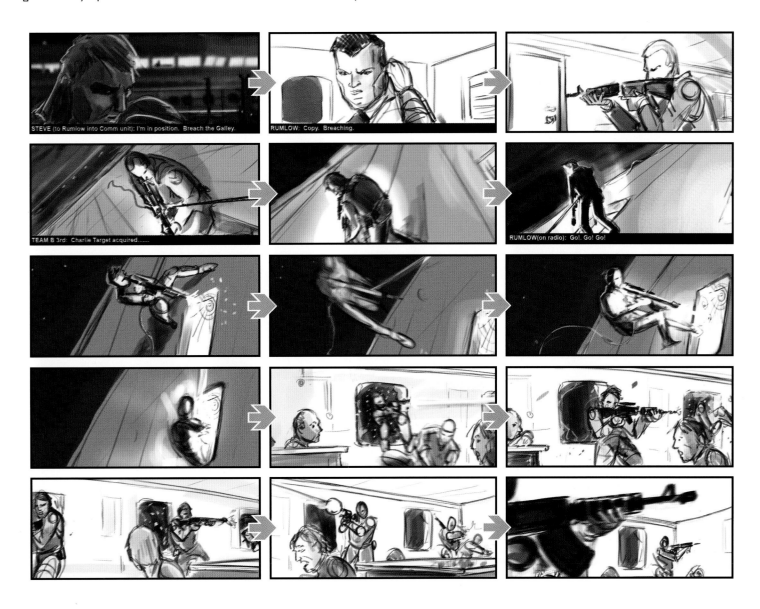

TEAM B LEADER(into radio): We're in!

SITWELL: I told you. SHIELD doesn't negotiate.

RADIO PIRATE(O.S.): .....Sir

RADIO PIRATE: .....The radio's dead.

BATROC: Merde--

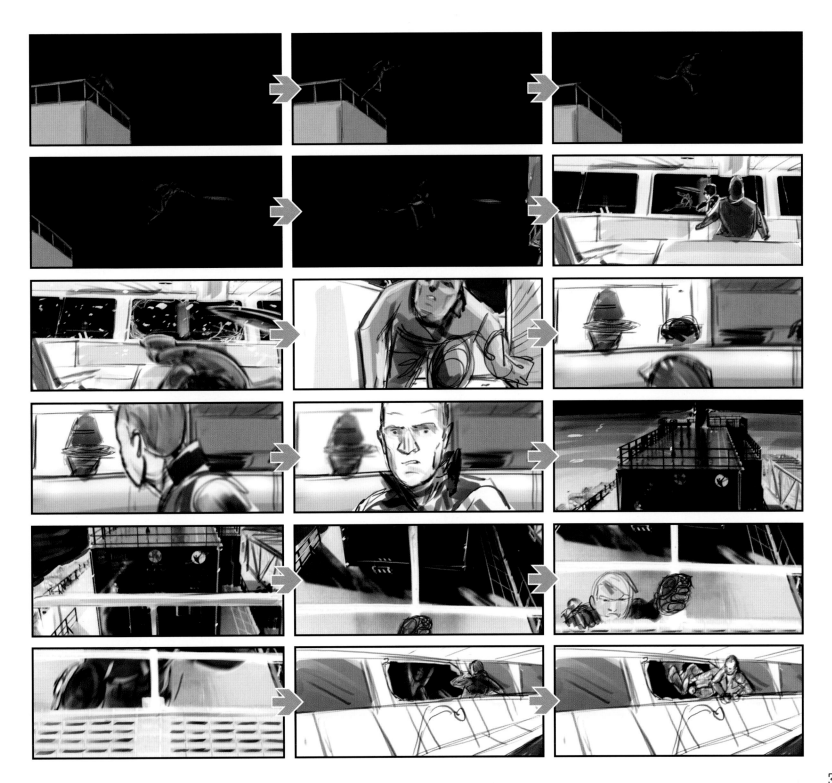

STEVE(into comm. unit): Rumlow.......

STEVE(into comm. unit): ......Get the hostages to the pods.......

STEVE(into comm. unit): ......Get the hostages to the pods.......

STEVE (into earpiece): Rumlow, you get that?

RUMLOW(on radio): We are on the move.

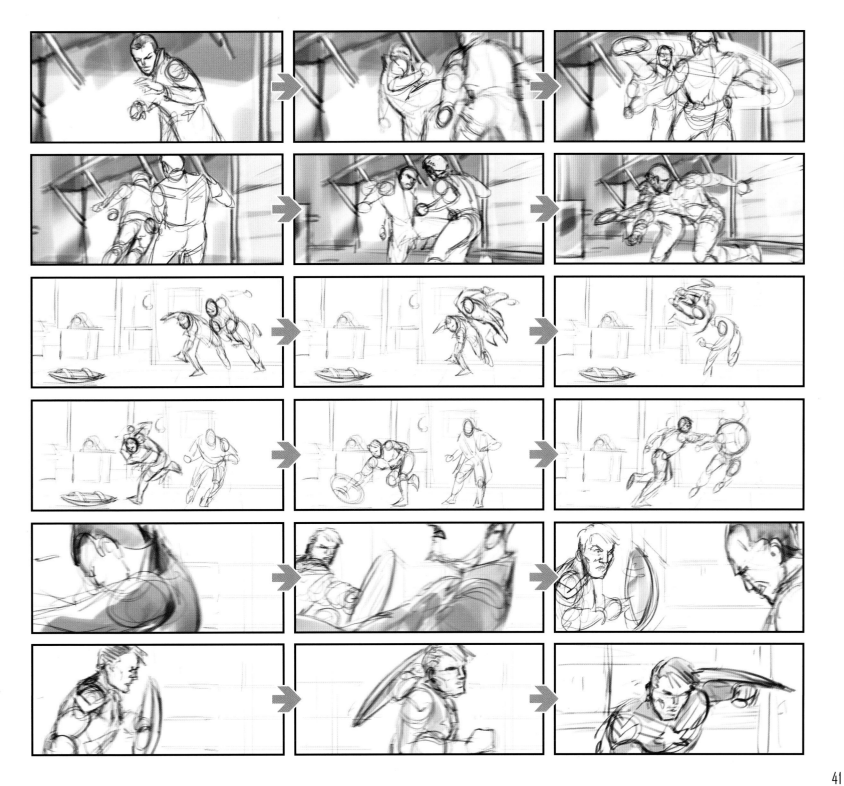

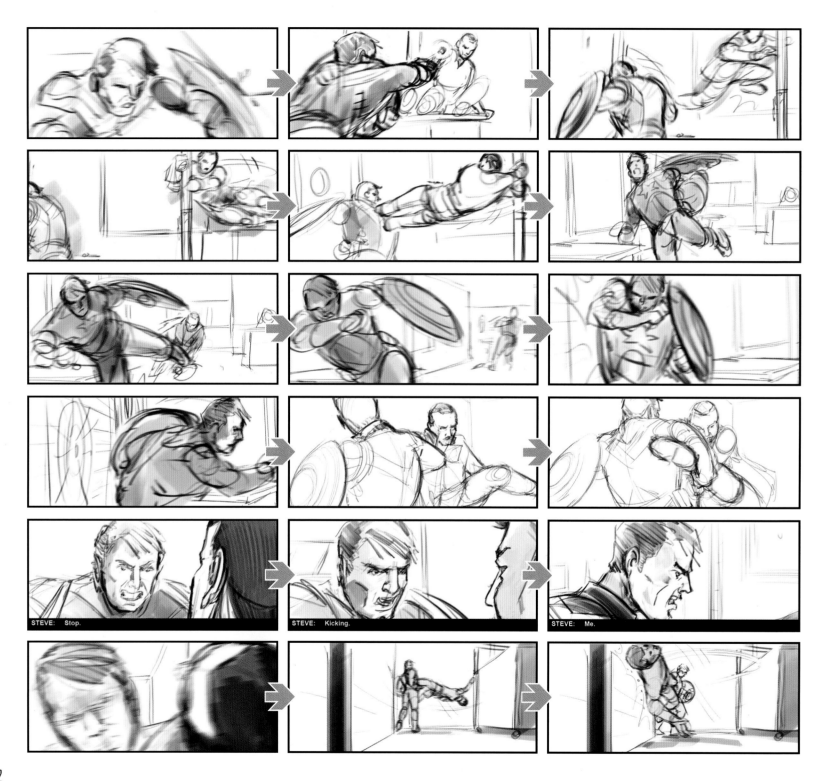

STEVE: Stop.

STEVE: Kicking.

STEVE: Me.

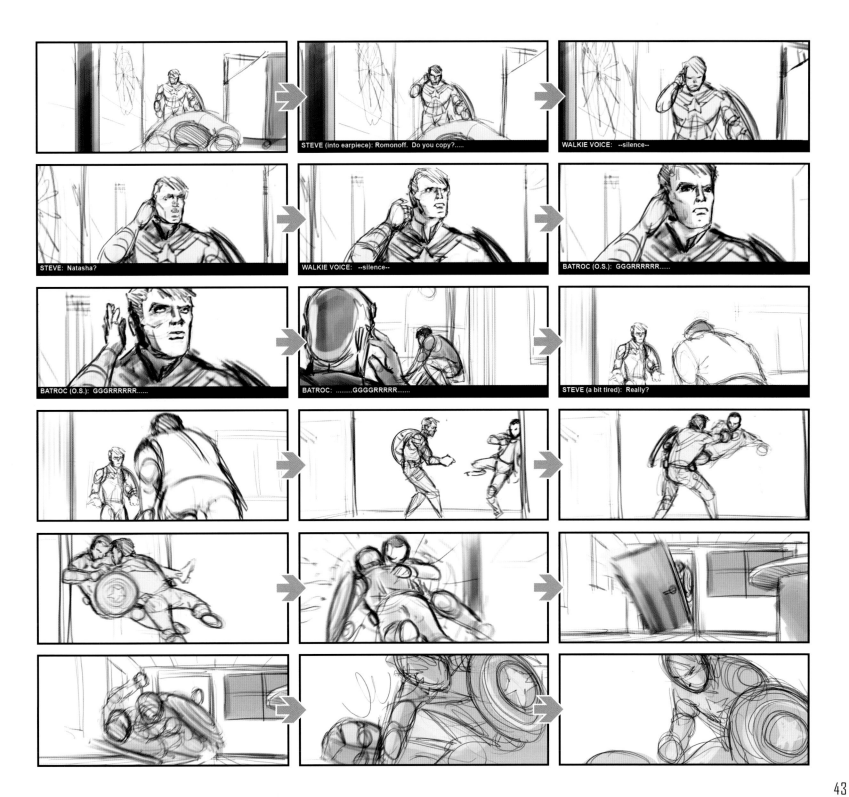

STEVE (into earpiece): Romonoff. Do you copy?.....

WALKIE VOICE: --silence--

STEVE: Natasha?

WALKIE VOICE: --silence--

BATROC (O.S.): GGGRRRRRR......

BATROC (O.S.): GGGRRRRRR......

BATROC: ....GGGGRRRRR.......

STEVE (a bit tired): Really?

"Cap knocks a door down using a bad guy as his battering ram," Concept Artist Rob McKinnon says. "Landing after that rough entrance. Cap is shocked to find Black Widow has already infiltrated the computer room and is gathering intel."

Everything is not as it seems on the Lemurian Star. Steve Rogers is living in a world he does not understand, a world of intrigue and conspiracy. His friends may be operating by their own rules, in shades of gray.

Victoria Alonso describes Black Widow's role in the scene: "Cap finds out something quite important about the Black Widow, which is the great reveal here."

Steve realizes that Natasha has been acting behind his back. Creative Executive Trinh Tran explains: "She's got a separate mission from Nick Fury—not everybody is as straightforward as he is."

Rob McKinnon keyframe.

44

Ryan Meinerding keyframe.

CHAPTER TWO
MAN OUT OF TIME

Captain America was the greatest hero of World War II. The living legend now stands in the long shadow of his past, adrift in the modern world. He visits his own memorial at the Smithsonian National Air and Space Museum, anonymously taking in the murals of his fallen comrades as he contemplates the fine line between freedom and fear, the simplicity of the past, and his future with S.H.I.E.L.D.

"It's such a sensitive and poignant moment in the story in terms of who Cap is and his back story with Bucky," Production Designer Peter Wenham says. "This was a great thing to be able to put together,

but there were limitations given the small amount of screen time that the exhibit has. The scene has an enormous scope to it, with Cap being who Cap is and with the moment being based in the Smithsonian in all its brilliance. Keeping the scope was important."

"It's a way for Cap to reconnect with the people he lost because everybody he knew in the forties, save one special person, has passed away—or so he thinks," Co-producer Nate Moore says. "It's kind of a somber moment."

CAPTAIN AMERICA
THE SYMBOL OF FREEDOM

"The murals were a unique challenge and took a really long time to paint," Marvel's Head of Visual Development Ryan Meinerding says. "They're printed enormous, and I've never painted anything that was meant to be printed so large. The one with all the Howling Commandos was printed about 25 feet tall and 60 feet wide, and had all the mannequins in costumes in front of it. The exhibit was real—they built it in a museum in Cleveland."

Meinerding says the murals also have a strong emotional presence: "The scene is also an introduction to Bucky. In painting the murals, I was trying to get as many moments between Cap and Bucky as possible. So you'll see Cap running with Bucky next to him or laughing with Bucky to reinforce the relationship they had."

Ryan Meinerding keyframe.

Producer Kevin Feige recalls strong memories of the Smithsonian: "Growing up in New Jersey I would go to Washington DC a lot on class trips, and my father would take me down there on holidays and weekends, and we'd go into the Smithsonian. The National Air and Space Museum in particular was part of my formative years. Not only my sense of history developed out of that, but also a sense of storytelling as it relates to history. So the fact that we actually got permission from the Smithsonian and shot there was sort of a childhood dream come true, or creative dream realized, for me, going back to those trips with my parents."

Peter Wenham explains his approach to the scene: "It's enormously important to afford at least one day—that's all I ask sometimes—at a real location, or have a real person in a real environment. All the connecting components come together then to create the illusion of Washington, D.C. I think we had one shot in the Smithsonian, which we negotiated for after hours. And that one shot in the real Smithsonian is so important because it just makes the credibility of what we created—Cap's exhibition in the Smithsonian—so much more believable."

Ryan Meinerding keyframe.

Wenham: "We ultimately built inside an existing automotive museum that hadn't been open that long, so there were sensitive issues there in terms of removing all the existing exhibits. But the reality in the journey through that exhibition is that I built my own environment within an environment. The only thing that it really gave me was the black ceiling with some spotlights. The actual journey through the Smithsonian as it is in the film was all built within there. The enormous curved wall with Cap on it and the flag in the background leading through to the iconic mannequins that are standing with the backdrop of Cap—that was all our own scenery built within an existing space.

"You could argue why not just use a stage, but a stage unfortunately wouldn't have worked. We kept the boundaries of working with existing architecture and with the ceiling in there. You just felt as if you were in a real exhibition space."

For Kevin Feige, the Smithsonian scenes have been a long time coming. "Since I started working at Marvel, I've always thought some day, if we bring Cap to present day, I want him to go to the Smithsonian and see relics from his own past," Feige says. "Because when I was a kid, I'd walk around the Smithsonian and think, what would the people who actually lived these experiences—

Ryan Meinerding keyframe.

the astronauts who came back, or the people who are long gone from World War II— what they would think of the exhibits. Is it being accurately reflected? Is it not? I always thought that was sort of interesting. And Cap is the only character where you can actually do that—have him come into his own exhibit."

Th...e ...nd Impact of

merica's Greatest Soldier

Set Designer David Moreau created 3-D renderings of the exhibit. "Ryan Meinerding had done two great initial concepts for the Howling Commandos—a more dynamic action-packed version and a more reflective version," Moreau says. "We went with the second concept to fit the more somber, reflective tone of the scene. Around the final Howling Commandos display, we built a whole exhibit space about Captain America and what he means as a symbol in today's United States of America. We played up some of the more nostalgic elements as a way to contrast against the disillusioned '70s-thriller tone of the story. He's a WWII-era action icon in a '70s thriller, and he has to return to his roots before he can rise to the occasion. The exhibit is designed to play up that difference."

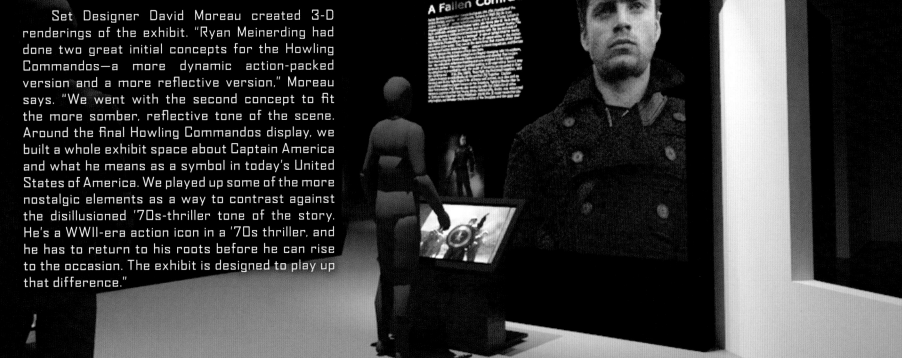

David Moreau 3-D renders.

Moreau: "The exhibit became about looking back to an earlier time to find the strength Cap needed to fight. It's a dark, reflective moment for Cap in the story. The exhibit had to not just reflect that, but also feel like he was journeying into his past—to before the current disillusion with S.H.I.E.L.D.—in order to find himself. The circular nature of the layout really helps make it feel like he's descending into his own past in order to find that strength."

Early Ryan Meinerding keyframe for a World War II-set opening sequence that was never filmed.

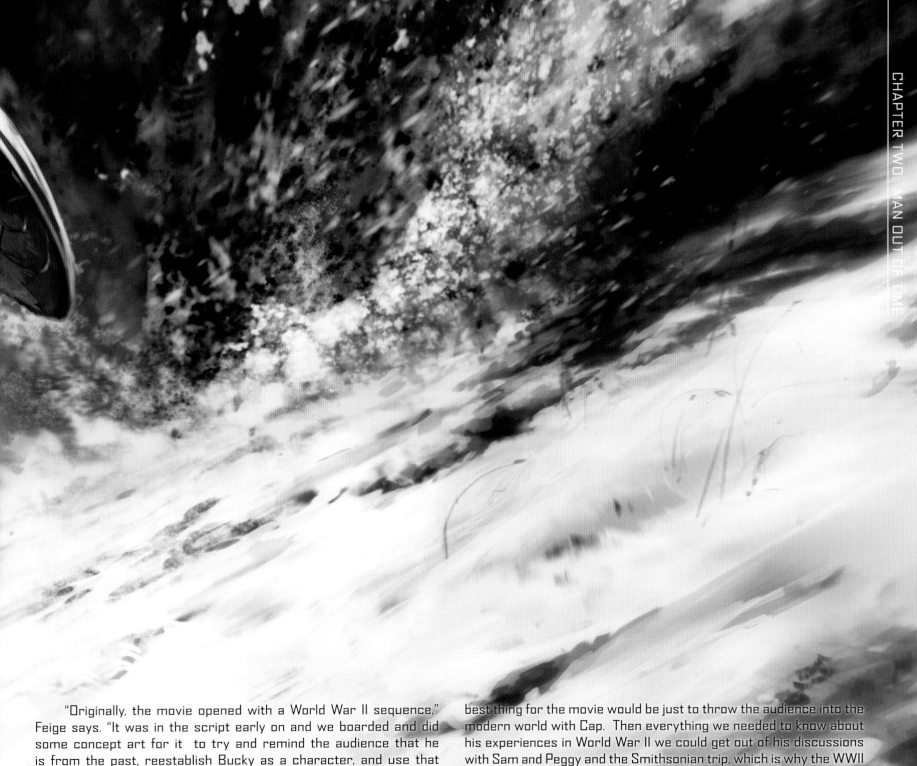

"Originally, the movie opened with a World War II sequence," Feige says. "It was in the script early on and we boarded and did some concept art for it to try and remind the audience that he is from the past, reestablish Bucky as a character, and use that to transition into the world. Before production, as we were going through it, we realized the Smithsonian served that purpose, and the best thing for the movie would be just to throw the audience into the modern world with Cap. Then everything we needed to know about his experiences in World War II we could get out of his discussions with Sam and Peggy and the Smithsonian trip, which is why the WWII sequence fell out of the film."

Early Ryan Meinerding keyframe for a World War II-set opening sequence that was never filmed.

While some of the props used were taken straight from the first film, the Captain America costume was not. Originally, Ryan Meinerding aspired to maintain the suit's look while solving some technical issues and improving its functionality. But then Producer Kevin Feige mentioned that Captain America had presumably possessed more than one suit during World War II.

"Kevin said we had seen a segment of the missions that Cap had gone on in WWII," Meinerding explains. "We didn't see all of them. He could have additional suits or have updated the suit himself."

Ryan Meinerding concept art.

Ryan Meinerding concept art.

"The suit Steve Rogers picks up in the Smithsonian is meant to represent the suit he used in WWII, but the actual suit he wore when he went into the ice was presumably damaged beyond repair," Meinerding continues. "Maybe it's in a more somber part of the exhibit, but this main costume on display is meant to foster idealist ideas about America and WWII—as well as being that red-white-and-blue iconic symbol of simple patriotism. We took a few liberties in updating the suit to be slightly more 'super hero,' though this movie is one of the more realistic takes on a super hero that Marvel has done. Injecting a little more super hero into that WWII suit was a welcome addition."

RYAN MEINERDING

CHAPTER THREE
WEB OF INTRIGUE

The Triskelion dominates the Washington, D.C., skyline, rising from the Potomac River to tower ominously over the centers of government and justice. S.H.I.E.L.D.'s headquarters is home not just to operations and advanced science but also to the slippery moral ambiguity of classified methods and secrets. Intelligence comes at a high price—maybe too high—and all may not be as it seems on this island of deceit.

In the comic-book Marvel Universe, the Triskelion is in New York. But for the movie, it exists on Theodore Roosevelt Island, a sliver of National Park Service land sandwiched between the neighborhood of Georgetown and the city of Arlington, Virginia. The actual site has been a park since Steve Rogers was a boy.

"The Triskelion isn't real, but we wanted a real landmass to build our imaginary building on top of," Co-producer Nate Moore explains.

The three-branched form of a triskelion is evident in the comic-book version's architecture, but that wasn't realistic given Roosevelt Island's long, narrow shape.

"One of the very important things to me and the directors was to ground everything in the film and base it in a true reality—a reality where you can believe there is a building of this size on Roosevelt Island," Production Designer Peter Wenham says. "We built the Triskelion to straddle the existing bridge that crosses Roosevelt Island. It was also enormously important to me to have something representative of a triskelion. And in the film, if you see a top shot looking at the main tower block, although it's round, there are three sides to it that actually form the shape of a triskelion."

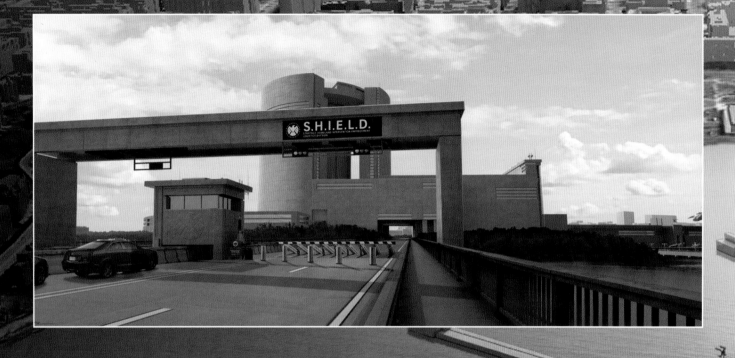

"We wanted the Triskelion to feel insular and fortress-like in addition to looking like a government building," Set Designer David Moreau says. "Peter Wenham, Concept Artist James Carson, and I went through quite a few different iterations on the central tower to try and find the one that best told the story. There are very few windows on the front, and most of the windows look inward on the Triskelion itself. S.H.I.E.L.D. is not an organization that lets anything in or out. This is a labyrinthine building full of secrets. It's also a little hard to grasp the size. We had to make sure to include reference points to show how massive this building was."

Concept art by James Carson & David Moreau.

CHAPTER THREE: WEB OF INTRIGUE

Carson worked with Moreau and Supervising Art Director Tom Valentine to refine Wenham's concept of the looming Triskelion foreshadowing S.H.I.E.L.D.'s excessive reach:

"In early explorations, Peter asked me to consider Brutalist and Nazi architecture styles, which lend themselves to the look we were trying to convey," Carson says. "This structure is a testament to the good things that can come from collaboration. I'm very pleased with how it turned out."

67

We found a newly reopened museum in Cleveland that had a giant, beautiful atrium, which is the atrium you'll see in the film. Peter based the design of the rest of the Triskelion around that atrium so he had something that was physical and tangible to anchor his design to." Nate Moore says.

James Carson concept art.

70

"The Triskelion is sort of Pentagon-meets-a-modern-building, so it's not as low-hanging and dated as the Pentagon structure," Moore says. "It's taller than any building in D.C. We break the D.C. rules about height limits, so the Triskelion lords over the rest of the skyline. It is something that is of the city. And in the stonework, texturally, it feels like it's part of the Capitol and Smithsonian and all those structures—but it's newer, a little slicker, and a little more modern."

Carson was tasked with dressing the entrance environment to match the rest of the Triskelion. "The entranceway illustration is based on the actual location where the scene was to be shot," he says.

HELICARRIER BAY

"The initial concept was written with five Helicarriers," Peter Wenham says. "Now anyone who knows the scale of a Helicarrier will want to know how you get five Helicarriers into a building on Roosevelt Island. That's when I decided the Helicarrier bay would be under the Potomac and there would be sluice gates that would open up, and floodgates would come out and doors pull back to reveal a bay underneath. But it was still too big, so we reduced it to three Helicarriers."

Three Helicarriers are two more than S.H.I.E.L.D. has had in past Marvel movies. Executive Producer and EVP of VFX and Post-Production Victoria Alonso describes the challenges of adding more Helicarriers.

"Is it harder to have three kids than two? Every one is different," Alonso says. "Just because you've done one, can you do three? Yes, of course. In different shots, does it become more cumbersome? Of course. Can you feature all of them? Yeah, you love your kids all the same, but some need special attention. The challenge is to keep it fresh and new."

Jamie Rama concept art.

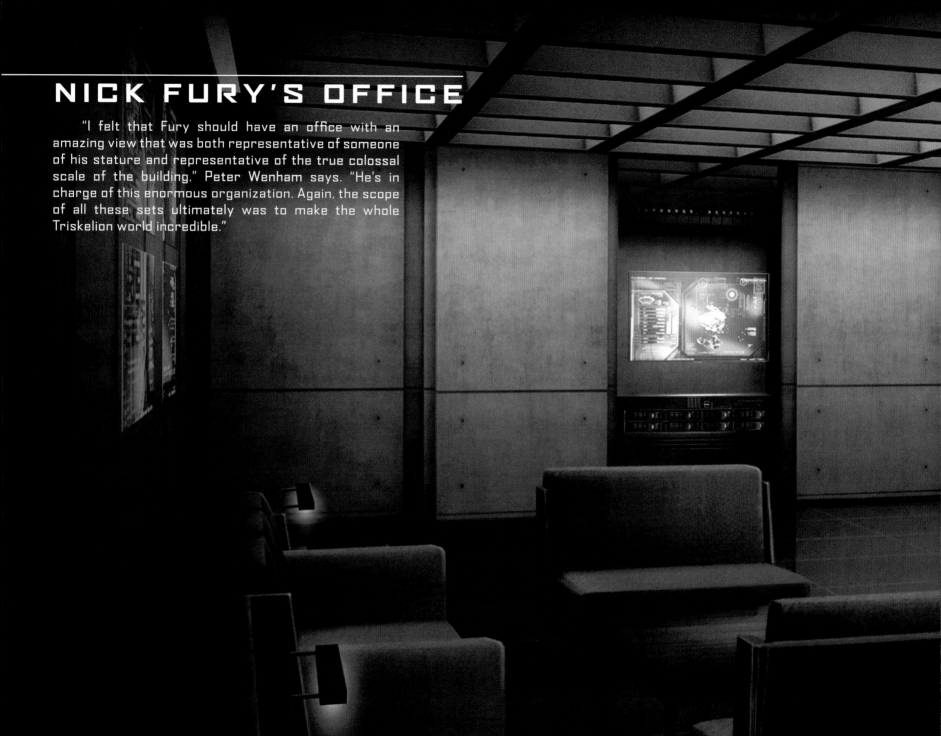

NICK FURY'S OFFICE

"I felt that Fury should have an office with an amazing view that was both representative of someone of his stature and representative of the true colossal scale of the building," Peter Wenham says. "He's in charge of this enormous organization. Again, the scope of all these sets ultimately was to make the whole Triskelion world incredible."

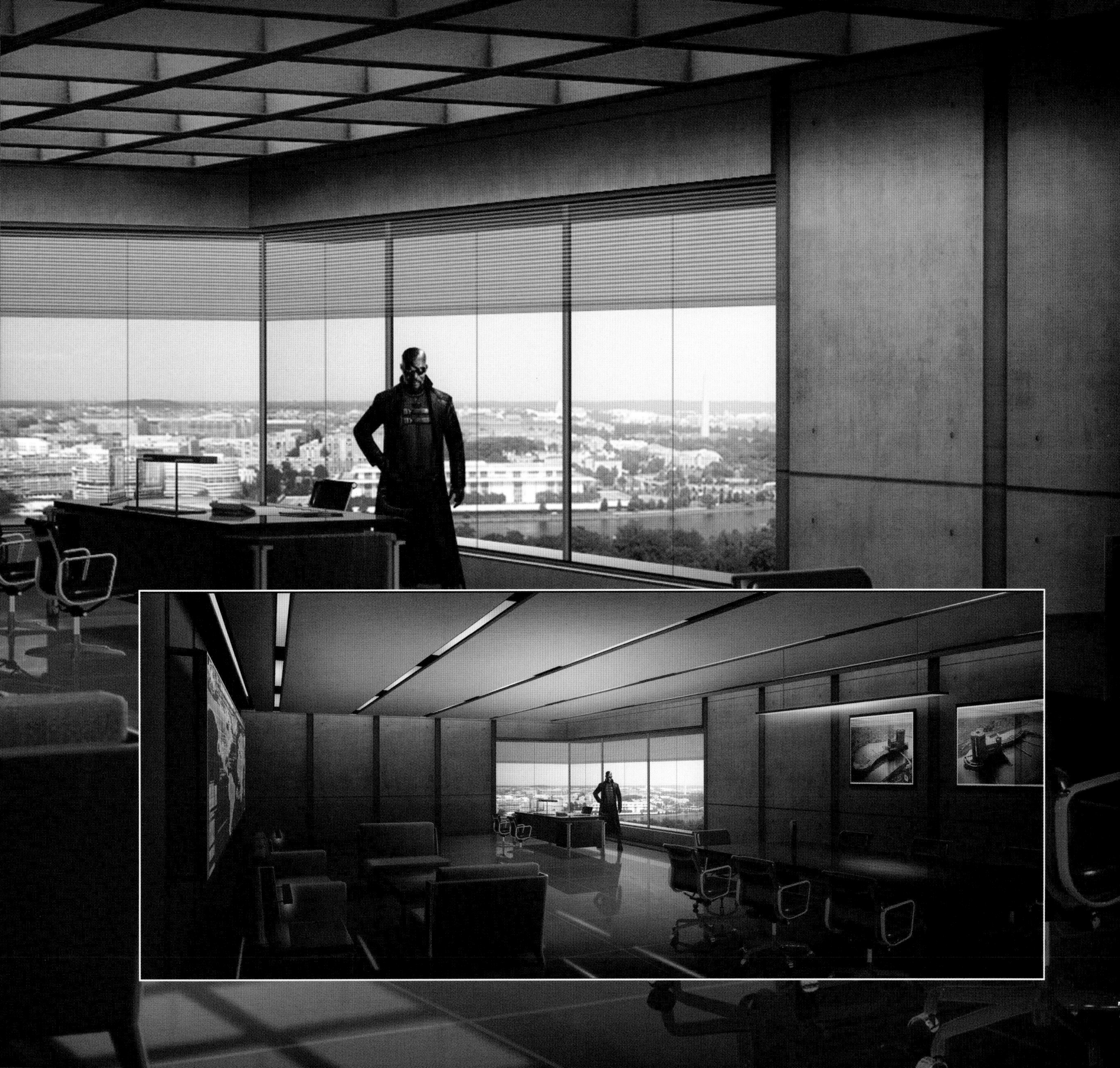

OPERATIONS CONTROL

Peter Wenham: "The Triskelion is colossal in its construction. But with the topography as it is, the challenge is to try to incorporate so many different components into this piece. There were many other facets besides what ends up in this film."

Jamie Rama concept art.

WORLD SECURITY COUNCIL

Jamie Rama concept art.

COMMUNICATIONS ANNEX

"At the far end of the Triskelion as it arcs around to the end of the island, there's a communications annex, which is where Cap takes over the internal communications," Peter Wenham says. "I anchored that in a position at the end because it had to be isolated from the main bulk of the building. If you think of a local TV station, and look at all the antennas and satellite dishes, it feels like that and is grounded in reality. It's important you believe this thing exists."

Jamie Rama concept art.

QUINJET LANDING PAD

"I wanted to incorporate the Quinjet pads into the Helicarrier bay, so we added blacktop aboveground to land the Quinjets," Peter Wenham says. "Just like conventional airplanes on military airfields, the Quinjets get wheeled over to a pad and then the pad hydraulically lowers down into the Helicarrier bay. There's a logic to everything."

Tim Flattery concept art.

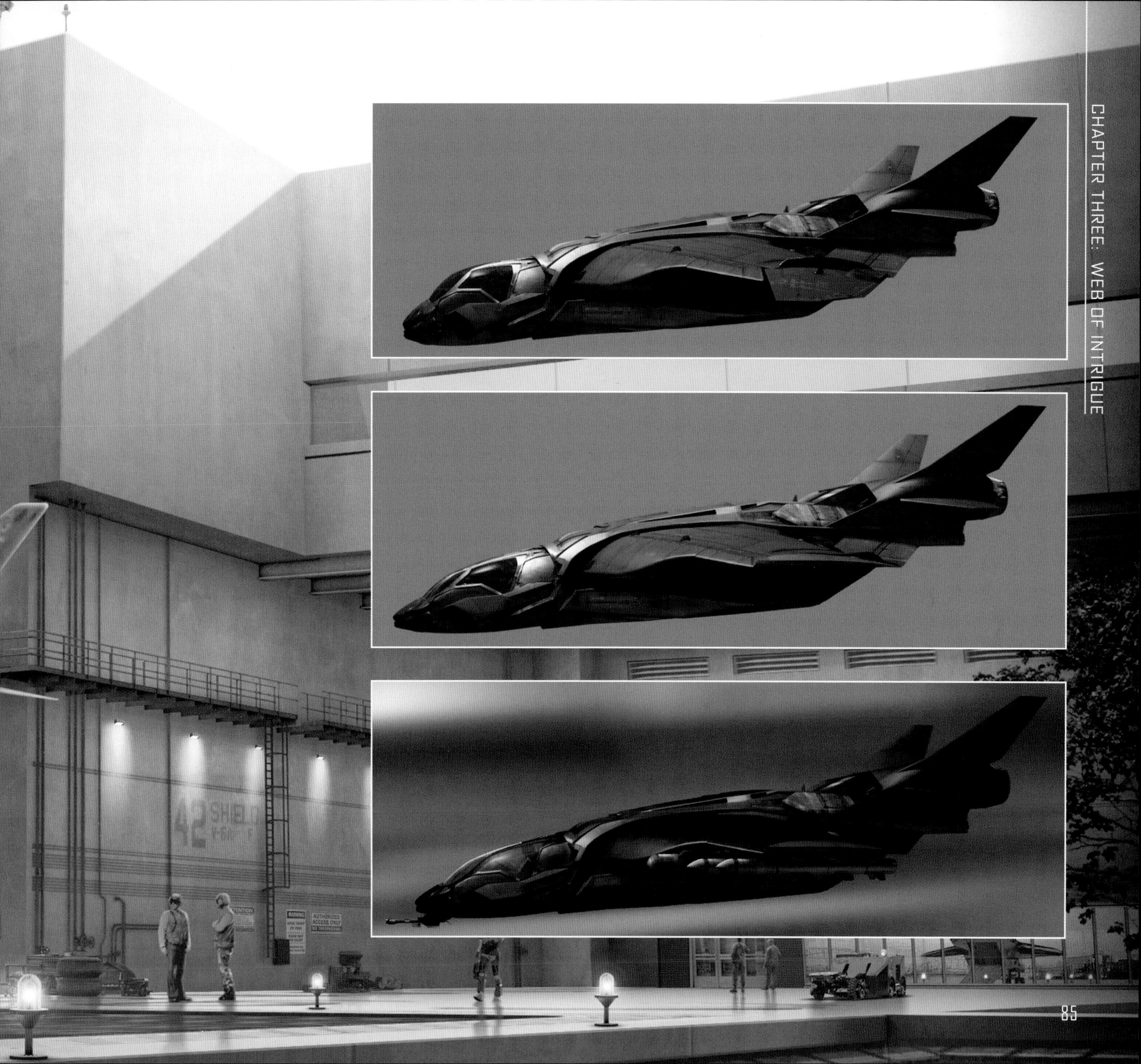
42

Industrial Light & Magic
digital model.

Jamie Rama concept art.

"Time has passed since the construction of the Helicarrier seen in the first *Avengers* movie," Set Designer Julien Pougnier says. "The new Helicarriers are updated with, among other things, surveillance hubs. They are shaped like reversed domes and are situated on the bottom of the Helicarriers. The hub is a surveillance device equipped with hundreds of ultra-high-tech cameras."

These cameras are powerful tools, but has S.H.I.E.L.D. overreached in its search for global intelligence?

"They can pinpoint anywhere on the planet down to the size of a postage stamp," Peter Wenham explains. "Think of Big Brother or Google Earth, then think of cameras that can locate almost anything."

David Marcou
concept art.

91

NICK FURY

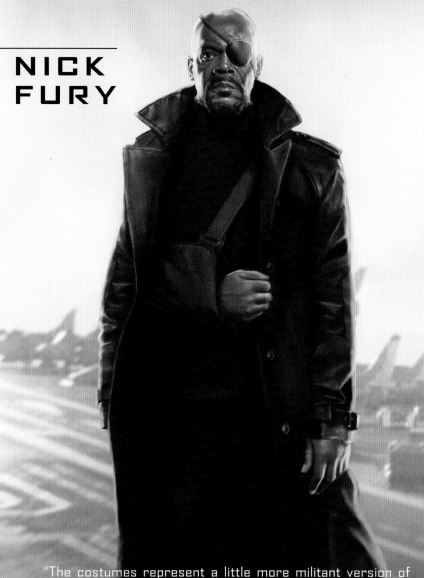

"The costumes represent a little more militant version of S.H.I.E.L.D.," Head of Visual Development Ryan Meinerding says. "Nick Fury is intended to look slightly fascist, like he might have gone too far in his attempts to protect the world."

Costume Illustrator Christian Cordella explains his work on Nick Fury's outfit: "Costume Designer Judianna Markovsky and I did so many different variations of colors, leather materials, seam patterns, position of pockets, until we found the right balance. It's subtle, but at the same time there is enough detail to become interesting. What is really important for this kind of a character is the silhouette. That determines the value of certain creations."

Christian Cordella concept illustration.

92

Executive Producer Louis D'Esposito describes Fury's look more succinctly: "Sam Jackson is the epitome of cool, so whatever he's doing—whatever role he's playing—you know he's going to be cool."

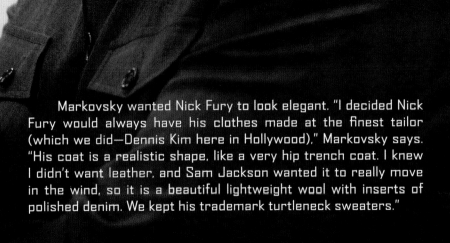

Markovsky wanted Nick Fury to look elegant. "I decided Nick Fury would always have his clothes made at the finest tailor (which we did—Dennis Kim here in Hollywood)," Markovsky says. "His coat is a realistic shape, like a very hip trench coat. I knew I didn't want leather, and Sam Jackson wanted it to really move in the wind, so it is a beautiful lightweight wool with inserts of polished denim. We kept his trademark turtleneck sweaters."

FURY'S SUV

Property Master Russell Bobbitt explains how he modified Nick Fury's armored SUV into a vehicle worthy of the head of S.H.I.E.L.D.: "The directors said it would be great to have a little machine gun come out of the center console. The gun part was easy, but the center console is a lot more challenging. We measured the real center console and determined the actual space was way too small for the gun we needed. We went to the drawing board."

Tim Flattery concept art.

94

Bobbitt: "We made the entire thing out of real steel, not rubber or plastic. This particular gun—the single piece—was about $65,000 to build. And we only had one. It came out really well, and it's a proud moment for the Props Department."

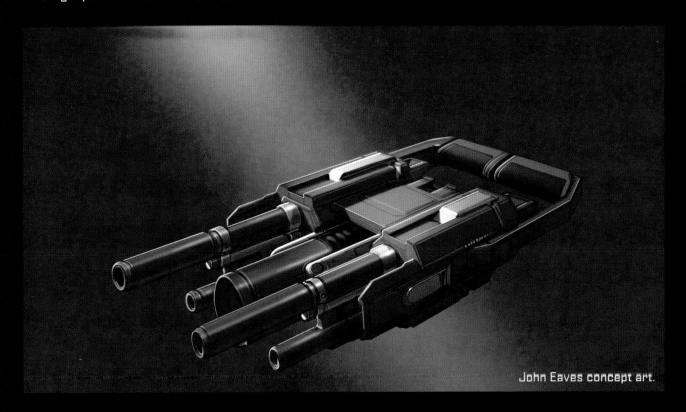

John Eaves concept art.

FURY CAR CHASE
STORYBOARDS BY DARRIN DENLINGER

Nick Fury has just called Maria Hill, instructing her to come to D.C. under deep-shadow conditions, when he is attacked by hostiles disguised as police officers.

"This was a small opening beat in a much larger action/chase sequence wonderfully orchestrated by Second Unit Director Spiro Razatos and his team," Storyboard Artist Darrin Denlinger says. "It's really nice to work on quieter character moments that are then punctuated by a big piece of action. My goal with the action was to create a fresh take on the overused 'T-bone crash' beat in which the camera is looking at a driver from the passenger seat of a car to shockingly reveal another car plowing into the driver's-side door. While incredibly effective in the first few movies that employed it, I don't think it really surprises audiences anymore."

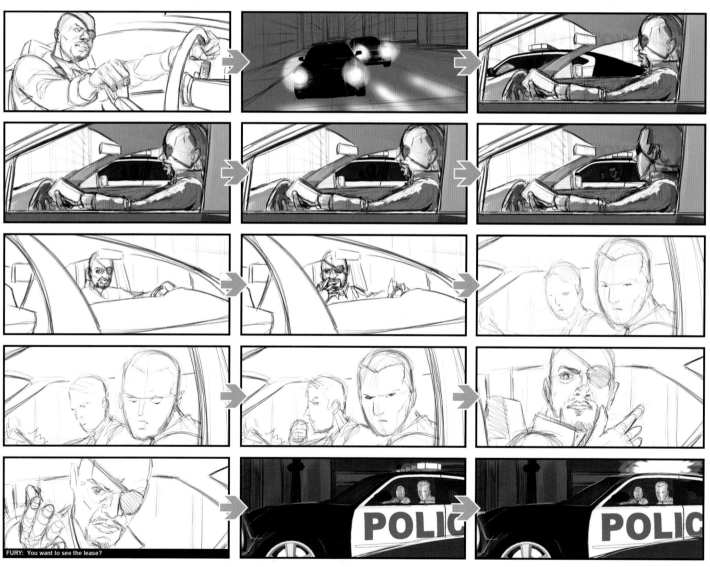

FURY: You want to see the lease?

"S.H.I.E.L.D. vehicles have a long history in the comics of being flight-capable, and we were able to hint at that when Fury discovers the flight system of his SUV is offline," Producer Kevin Feige says.

Rob McKinnon keyframes with production still (top left).

WARNING

STEVE'S APARTMENT

Peter Wenham describes developing living quarters for Steve Rogers: "You could argue that Cap should live within the Triskelion, as he's S.H.I.E.L.D.'s most expensive asset. But one of the challenges with Cap is he needs to be human. In the contemporary world, he needs to be liked, to be cool, to be grounded in reality as a normal guy living in everyday society—even though he has these special abilities.

"We could have given him a great big high-tech apartment with lovely views of Washington, D.C. But then we veered toward something that made him so vulnerable and transparent given who he is. We moved him into a red-brick, third-floor apartment near Dupont Circle."

James Carson's illustrations helped bring Steve Rogers' apartment to life. "His apartment, like him, is a little unsettled," Carson says. "Add his personality as a no-frills, practical man, and we would not see a great deal of flourish."

James Carson concept art.

Wenham: "Tonality-wise, Steve Rogers is very regimented and organized in his approach to things because of his military training. He still polishes his shoes and leaves them at the foot of his bed like he did when he was a recruit in the Army. He lines everything up accordingly. There's no mess. Everything has structure. All the components in his apartment are organized and regimented. He's very systematic about how he goes about his day.

"There's also a bit of fun in there—he's a character who is learning. He's been asleep, cocooned, for the last 70 years. He's learning about the Beatles, and computers—all that stuff we take for granted."

Steve Rogers does have certain areas of interest, and it shows. "Knowledge is very important to him, so his library is set up and functional," Carson says. "We see hints of the things he loves, among them his country and his motorcycle."

James Carson concept art.

Ryan Meinerding roughed out the scene in which Captain America finds Nick Fury taking shelter in his living room. "My process has always been to start in grayscale, and then I'd color," Meinerding says. "And in the past, I'd have a little more time to work on the grayscale, so I'd turn in a more finished grayscale. A lot of the work I did on the first *Iron Man* was like that, but then people needed answers to simple questions—like 'What does Iron Man look like when he walks?', 'What does Iron Man look like when he flies?', 'What does Iron Man look like in a dark room?'

Ryan Meinerding concept art.

"And as we've gone through the movies, everyone has the answers to those questions in their heads now, so they don't ask them anymore," Meinerding continues. "The questions they ask as we work on the keyframes become more and more specific, and we can't just stay in grayscale most times because we have to communicate all the information out there in the keyframes."

"I really like working in grayscale," Meinerding says. "I find it easier to get ideas out that way. With the Nick Fury stuff, I was aiming to get a lot of keyframes done relatively quickly. But also, the gray sets the tone as being a little bit darker, and the red blood helps stamp the significance and power of that moment. I would have liked to have gone back and colored the whole thing, but it would have stayed pretty dark and monochromatic until he was shot."

Ryan Meinerding
keyframe.

Ryan Meinerding keyframe.

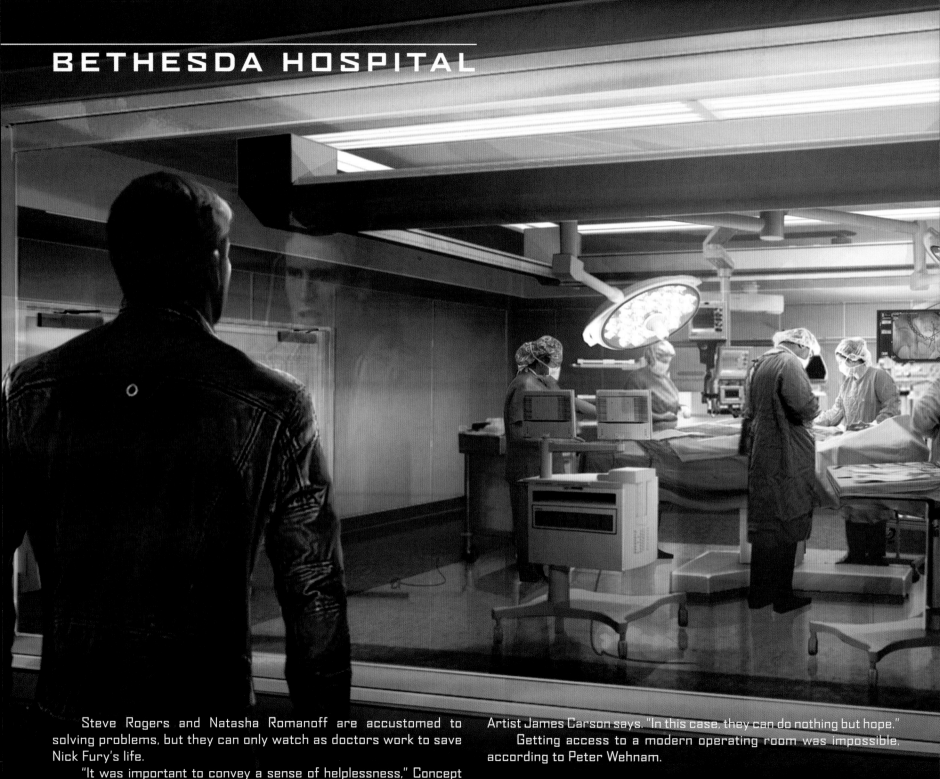

BETHESDA HOSPITAL

Steve Rogers and Natasha Romanoff are accustomed to solving problems, but they can only watch as doctors work to save Nick Fury's life.

"It was important to convey a sense of helplessness," Concept Artist James Carson says. "In this case, they can do nothing but hope."

Getting access to a modern operating room was impossible, according to Peter Wehnam.

James Carson concept art.

"We found a hospital—St. Vincent's in downtown L.A.—that worked perfectly, but shooting a scene in an operating theater is always a non-starter, and old ones are small and tired," he says.

"I built the operating theater because I wanted a letterbox window. We actually played the whole scene looking into the theater from a viewing room with this enormous rectilinear window, which I was quite keen on building into the set as a window into the world of Fury. You'd never find that in a real environment. There's a lot of rectilinear work in the overall concept and how I approached everything in the movie, aside from the Triskelion."

CHAPTER FOUR
FIGHT OR FLIGHT

"Don't trust anyone." Nick Fury's final warning echoes through Steve Rogers' mind as the Acting Director of S.H.I.E.L.D., Alexander Pierce, grimly details his suspicions regarding Fury's surreptitious actions.

Only moments later, Captain America has an opportunity to reconsider Fury's words as S.H.I.E.L.D. agents attack in the Triskelion elevator. Cap must fight for his freedom before escaping underground in his search for clues to unravel this tangled political conspiracy. Where does Alexander Pierce fit into the web of intrigue and corruption?

"In our film, Alexander Pierce is Nick Fury's mentor, almost the man who made Fury the head of S.H.I.E.L.D.," Co-producer Nate Moore says. "And we thought that was interesting because as the mystery unfolds, you realize that maybe Pierce did that for a very specific reason, and that reason is not the same as what Fury thought it was."

And what about Black Widow? Who is the real Natasha? Does she even know?

"There's a pretty good distinction in the film of what it means to be a soldier, versus what it means to be a spy," Moore continues. "What it means to believe in something and to fight for what is right, versus operating in shades of gray all the time, and what sacrifices you make personally with either of those choices."

Though their ideologies and agendas sometimes differ, both Captain America and Black Widow are loyal to Nick Fury. But to find his assassin, they must stay out of S.H.I.E.L.D.'s crosshairs.

TRISKELION ESCAPE
PRE-VISUALIZATION BY MONTY GRANITO

"For this sequence, all we got was the concept art," says Monty Granito, Previsualization Supervisor at Proof, Inc. "VFX Supervisor Dan DeLeeuw let us run with it a bit, telling us Cap had to get to the other side of the Quinjet and he had to hit it with the shield. The feel was Cap slaying a dragon.

"That's the way it goes in previs a lot of times: You get an image

with pertinent story beats, then see what you can comte up with. If there's something good there, the rest of the time will be shaping it to enhance the director's vision. I did a first pass to get feedback from the VFX Supervisor and directors. I created a moment where the Quinjet bucks Cap off and Cap hits the other wing with his shield to stay on. That's the cool part about fighting a dragon—staying on top of it."

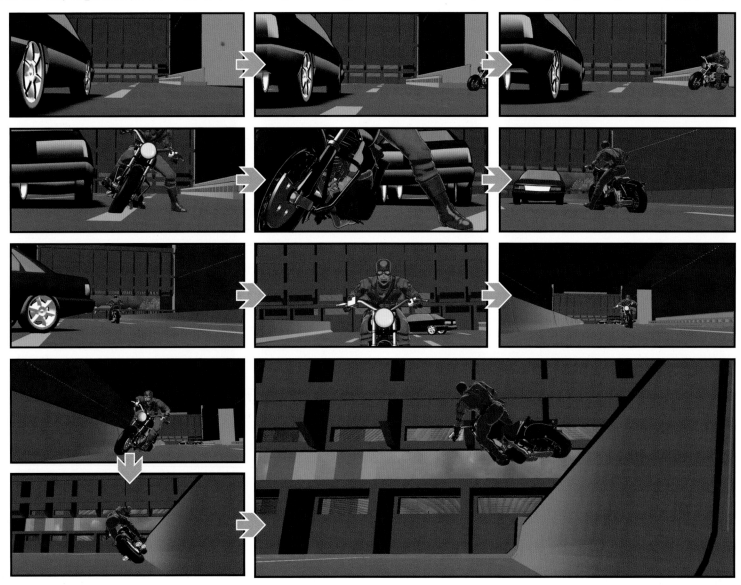

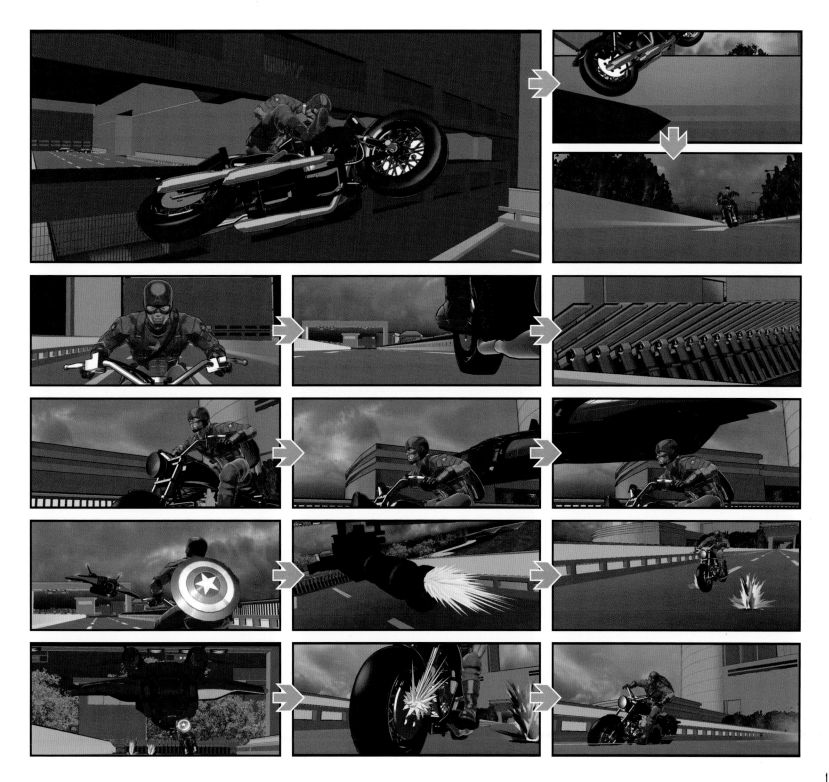

Granito: "Cap had to take down the Quinjet efficiently so it wouldn't hurt innocent people. Dan wanted as much mayhem as possible, and the directors want to keep Cap athletically amazing but always grounded, so we took all of those things into consideration.

"For the final leap, I gave the shot to my colleague Tom Bruno, who was very good at animating off of the gymnastic reference they were giving us. Tom did a great job of making Cap feel graceful and powerful in that final moment of crashing the shield down. We used an amalgam of gymnastics, parkour, and comic-book poses to come up with Cap's movements.

"Marvel is extraordinary in its passionate protection of its characters. In action sequences, it can be easy to let heroes do things against their character for the sake of the story. Marvel doesn't do that. Every action has to be one the character would actually think about and do. As a comic-book nerd myself, that is very refreshing."

Rodney Fuentebella keyframe.

VFX Producer Jen Underdahl realized early on that the only real parts of the Quinjet sequence would be Cap—first on his bike, then grabbing his shield, dismantling the remaining engines, and leaping to safety. "The Art Department and Special Effects teamed up to build us a 'buck' of the Quinjet to scale so that all of the actor's footfalls would closely approximate our CG version, allowing us to replace one for the other," Underdahl says. "We painted the Quinjet gray so that natural light would bounce off our actor. In close-ups of Chris interacting with the canopy or shield, the Art Department supplied us with the real thing.

"Scanline VFX built and textured a CG Quinjet, based on approved designs. They created a digital double of Captain America and digitally modeled the motorcycle he uses to make his escape. Having pre-built and pre-planned all aspects of this sequence allowed the directors to improvise on the spot if they wanted to veer from the previs, and the planning allowed us to have maximum freedom to put the pieces together once we received a cut from Editorial. In most of the shots, aside from Cap and his bike, the rest has been entirely conceived and constructed by a group of super-talented CG artists."

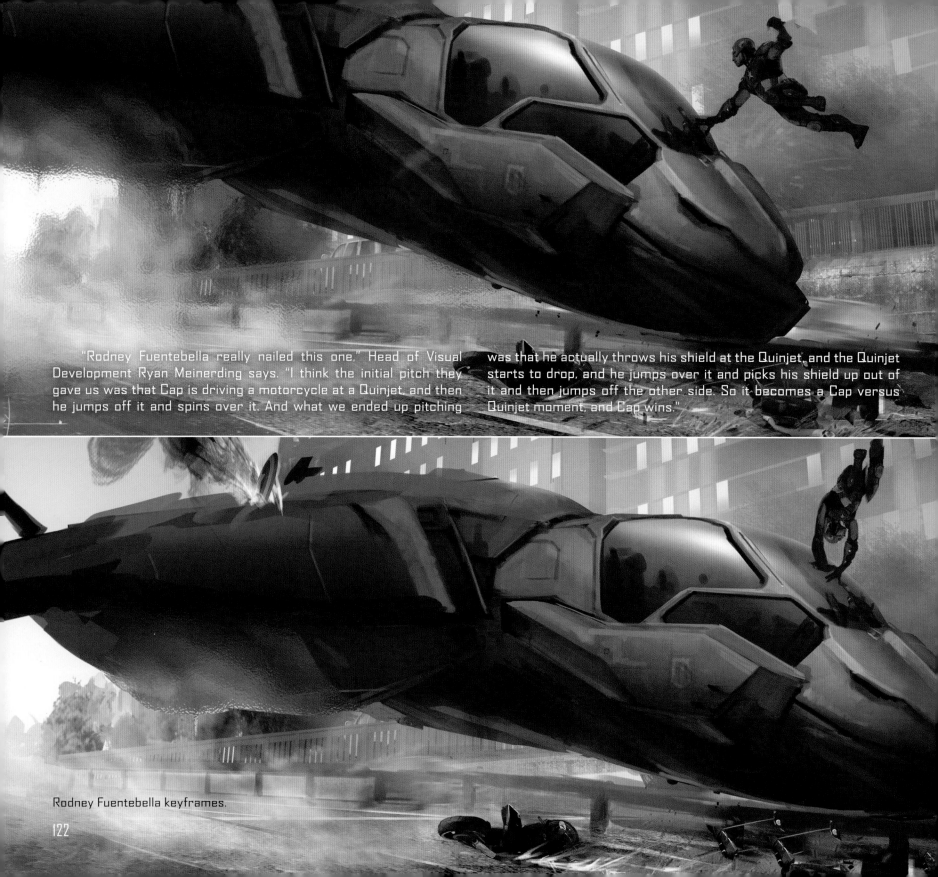

"Rodney Fuentebella really nailed this one," Head of Visual Development Ryan Meinerding says. "I think the initial pitch they gave us was that Cap is driving a motorcycle at a Quinjet, and then he jumps off it and spins over it. And what we ended up pitching was that he actually throws his shield at the Quinjet, and the Quinjet starts to drop, and he jumps over it and picks his shield up out of it and then jumps off the other side. So it becomes a Cap versus Quinjet moment, and Cap wins."

Rodney Fuentebella keyframes.

"I wanted to show Captain America taking on an impossible foe—in this case, a Quinjet—with heroic intent," Concept Artist Rodney Fuentebella says. "I wanted the audience to feel that even with the size difference, Cap is still willing to take on a fully armed jet. And, eventually, he takes it down."

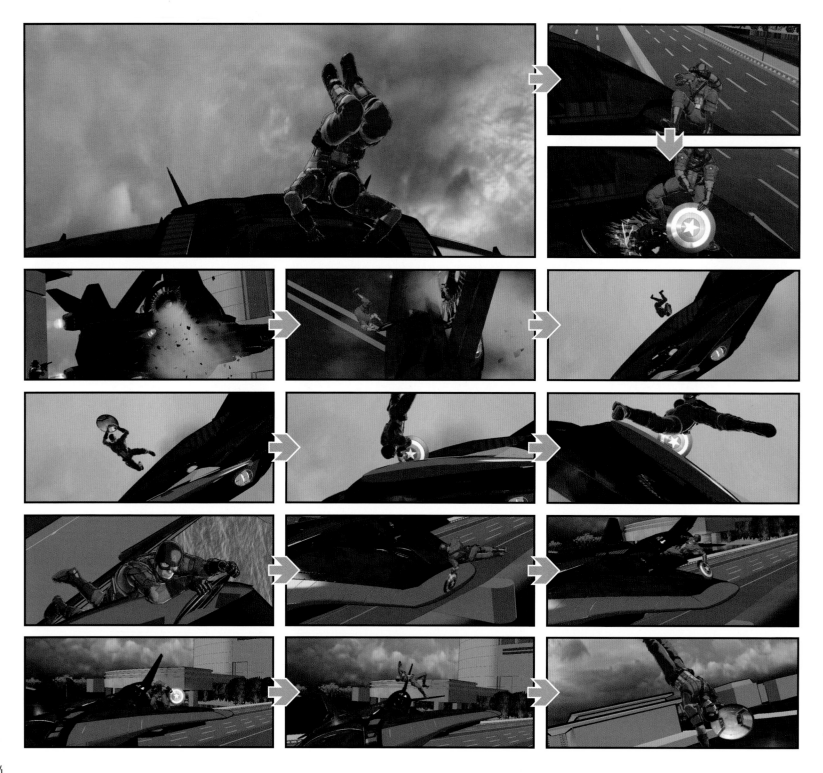

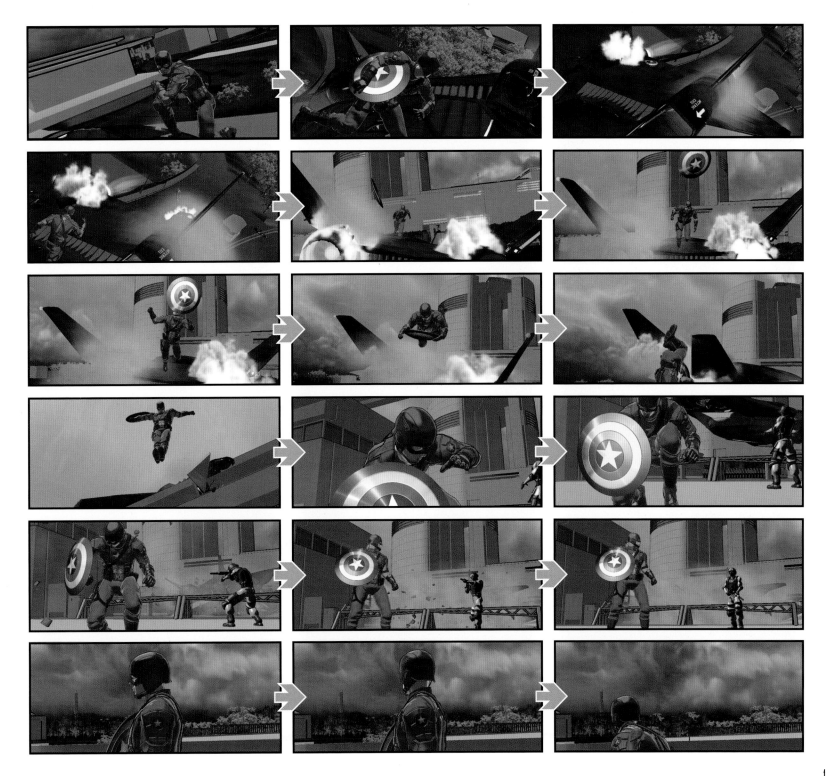

CAMP LEHIGH

The search for information leads Steve Rogers and Natasha Romanoff to Camp Lehigh, a location fundamental to Captain America's origins.

"In the first movie, Steve was trained at Camp Lehigh," Creative Executive Trinh Tran explains. "He became a soldier there. We wanted him to relive that moment."

But like the world at large, the Army base moved on while Steve was gone.

"What's interesting is when he returns, he finds that Camp Lehigh isn't exactly how he left it," Nate Moore says. "Like any camp, it advanced over time. And even as a defunct camp, it still has structures that weren't there when he trained in the '40s, because it's moved forward with time. But the scene still hints at a time he is a little wistful for, when things seemed a little bit simpler. However, what he finds at Camp Lehigh is something that is unexpected and ends up tying into the very modern and present-day problem that he's facing."

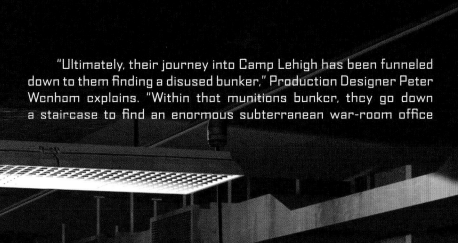

"Ultimately, their journey into Camp Lehigh has been funneled down to them finding a disused bunker," Production Designer Peter Wenham explains. "Within that munitions bunker, they go down a staircase to find an enormous subterranean war-room office where operations would have taken place back in WWII. The scope and look of the base ultimately became a visual effect anchored onto two existing buildings, some walkways, and a façade that we built using the old Sears factory in downtown Los Angeles."

Jamie Rama concept art.

129

Set Designer Anshuman Prasad created 3-D renders of the bunker, then enhanced by Illustrator Jamie Rama, while Concept Artist Christopher Ross worked on the individual computer units. "It was a very challenging design, as the set had to convey a sense of being old and technologically archaic, yet also fit into the Marvel world of a fantasy super-hero movie," Prasad says. "Together with Peter Wenham and Supervising Art Director Thomas Valentine, we went though a number of designs—starting from a circular well, to radial banks of computers, to finally settle on a large parking-garage-like space. I think the vast and open space with endless banks of data processors and a low ceiling was what helped convey the enormity and scale that the script called for. After all, though technologically archaic now, we had to present it as cutting edge at the time it was supposed to have been built, in the mid- to late '60s."

Jamie Rama concept art with production still (inset).

CAMP LEHIGH ESCAPE
STORYBOARDS BY DARRIN DENLINGER

"The Camp Lehigh section is important because it firmly entrenches the film as a throwback to the political thrillers of the 1970s, rather than placing it within the structure of a traditional super-hero film," Storyboard Artist Darrin Denlinger says. "The Russo brothers hammered this concept home from our very first meetings. It influenced how I approached each scene, looking for any visual opportunity to rachet up a sense of unease and distrust with established authority figures in the film's world."

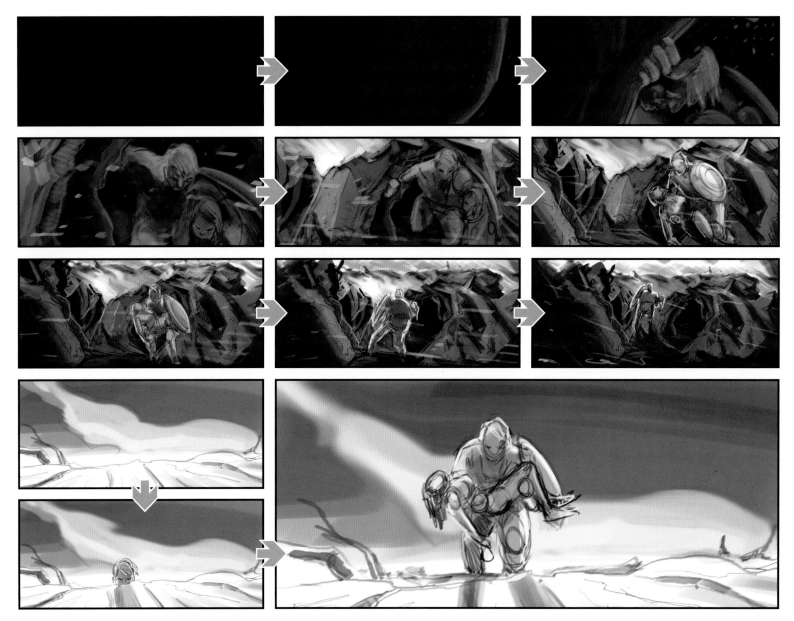

Andrew Kim keyframe.

"The Camp Lehigh section shows Natasha and Steve on their own and on the run, uncovering a long-standing network of evil that has poisoned the highest levels of S.H.I.E.L.D., much like Faye Dunaway and Robert Redford's journey in *Three Days of the Condor*—except with Quinjets, a Vibranium shield, and missile attacks," Denlinger adds.

Andrew Kim keyframe.

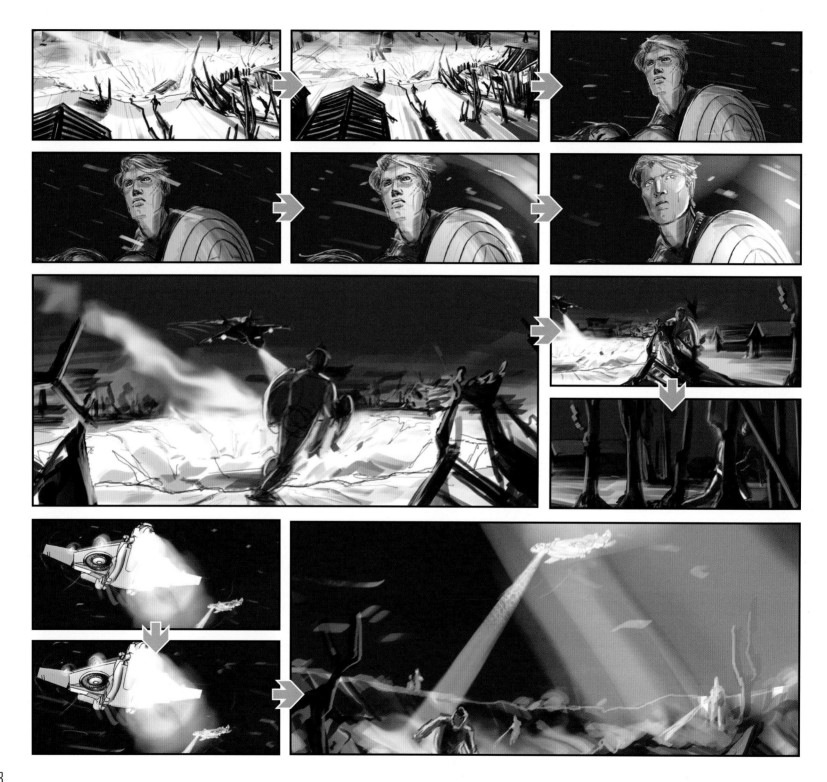

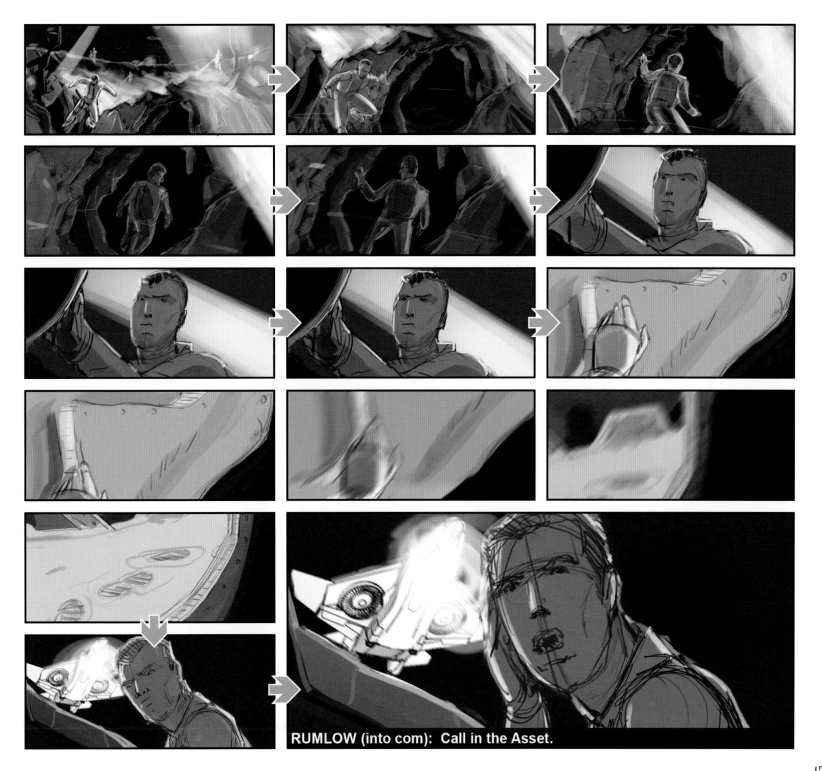

RUMLOW (into com): Call in the Asset.

CHAPTER FIVE
WINTER KILLS

Steve Rogers' past collides with his present when the masked operative known as the Winter Soldier ambushes the car in which Steve, Sam, and Natasha are traveling. S.H.I.E.L.D. Agent Jasper Sitwell, in the back seat, is brutally plucked from their midst by an unseen hand. The three heroes are taken by surprise, unable to see their assailant from within the car's claustrophobic confines; they are then separated in the ensuing strike.

Black Widow takes on the man beneath the mask first. "The battle on the roadway is a great scene," Concept Artist Rodney Fuentebella says. "I wanted the chaos and destruction to encircle Black Widow and Winter Soldier."

Moments later, Captain America joins the fray. Then suddenly— shockingly—his rendezvous with the past is revealed. The man out of time is faced with the horror of truth.

But he is not alone.

"With Winter Soldier, Directors Joe and Anthony Russo really wanted a strong icon that was just scary. It was like they wanted to create the next Darth Vader or Boba Fett," Head of Visual Development Ryan Meinerding says. "And they talked about it with such passion that it was kind of intimidating to work on, because I never went into a meeting thinking, 'Oh yeah, I've nailed the next Boba Fett.' They really wanted Winter Soldier to be a threat to Cap, and to be dangerous and resonate and stay in people's minds like those villains have."

WINTER SOLDIER

Ryan Meinerding concept art.

Marvel's Visual Development team was tasked with designing the Winter Soldier, bringing Captain America's elusive foe from comics to screen.

"Whenever we design a character, we start with the comics," Ryan Meinerding explains. "Steve Epting's design for Winter Soldier is fantastic. We really were looking to translate it as much as we could, and just add detail and make it work for the needs of the story. In Winter Soldier's design in both the comics and the movie, his long hair is a classic convention to show that time has passed. Other than that, we had three touchstones."

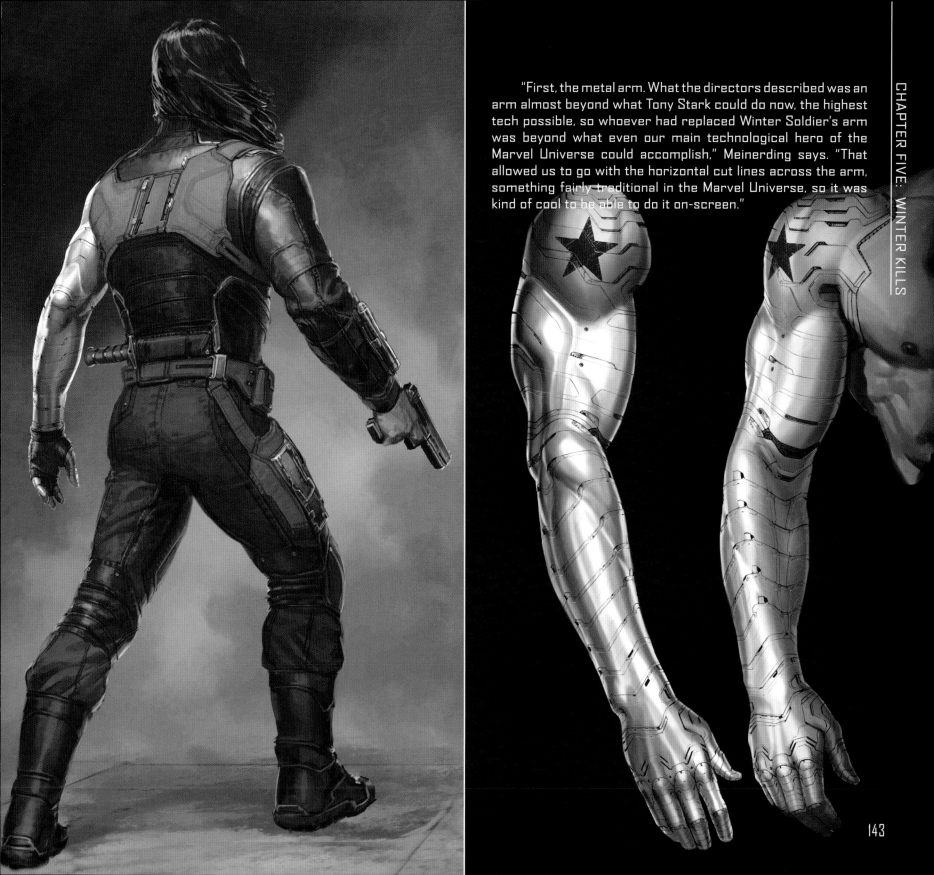

"First, the metal arm. What the directors described was an arm almost beyond what Tony Stark could do now, the highest tech possible, so whoever had replaced Winter Soldier's arm was beyond what even our main technological hero of the Marvel Universe could accomplish," Meinerding says. "That allowed us to go with the horizontal cut lines across the arm, something fairly traditional in the Marvel Universe, so it was kind of cool to be able to do it on-screen."

"Second, the mask," Meinerding continues. "The domino mask stretches back to Bucky's comic-book roots. We did different variations—whether it was face paint or goggles or a full mask, we needed some way to conceal Winter Soldier's identity for a portion of the movie when the audience and Steve weren't supposed to recognize him. Unfortunately, it's just really hard to do a domino mask because it doesn't fit with anything that we think of as the real world. The closest we got was actually doing face paint, but I'm still excited we got something that resembled the domino mask."

Ryan Meinerding concept art.

Meinerding: "The final touchstone for the Winter Soldier was the Russo brothers' distinct desire to make him as cool a villain as possible. Visual Development has had to design quite a few Marvel villains up to this point, and we are always trying to find ways to make villains interesting and relatable."

Rodney Fuentebella concept art.

146

Rodney Fuentebella describes his approach: "From something sleek and modern to something paramilitary, then to a more rebel look—we wanted to try all types in order to see if the design could work with the idea of the Winter Soldier."

147

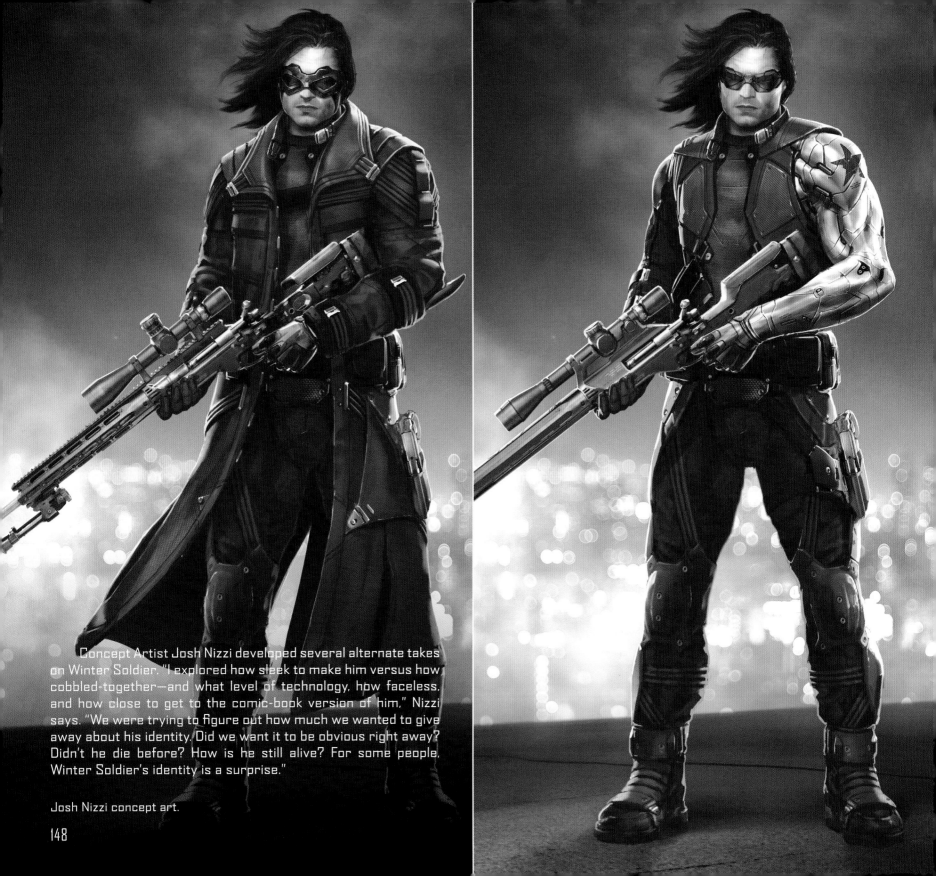

Concept Artist Josh Nizzi developed several alternate takes on Winter Soldier. "I explored how sleek to make him versus how cobbled-together—and what level of technology, how faceless, and how close to get to the comic-book version of him," Nizzi says. "We were trying to figure out how much we wanted to give away about his identity. Did we want it to be obvious right away? Didn't he die before? How is he still alive? For some people, Winter Soldier's identity is a surprise."

Josh Nizzi concept art.

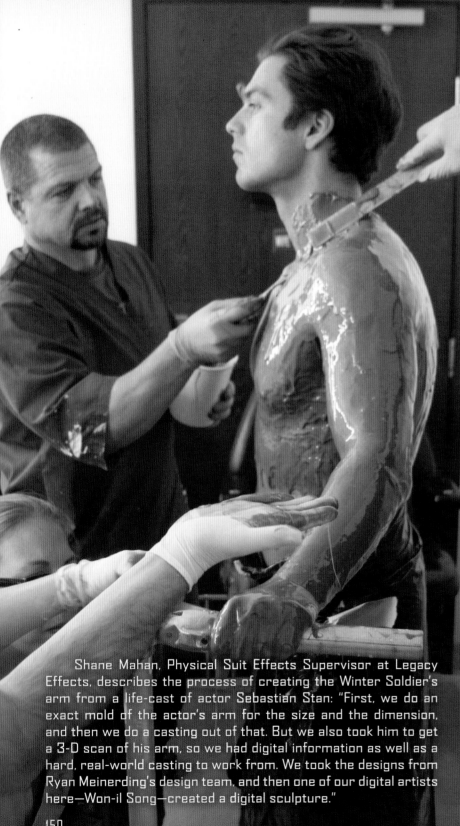

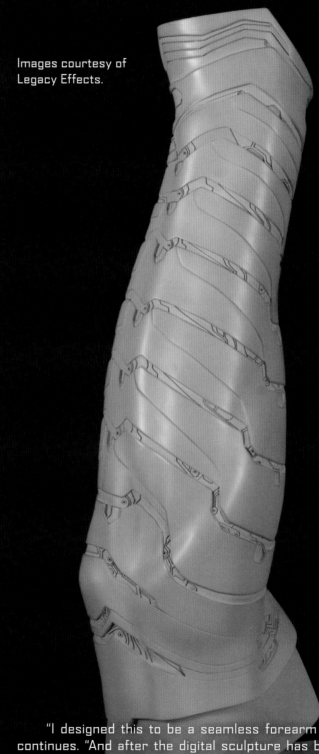

Images courtesy of Legacy Effects.

Shane Mahan, Physical Suit Effects Supervisor at Legacy Effects, describes the process of creating the Winter Soldier's arm from a life-cast of actor Sebastian Stan: "First, we do an exact mold of the actor's arm for the size and the dimension, and then we do a casting out of that. But we also took him to get a 3-D scan of his arm, so we had digital information as well as a hard, real-world casting to work from. We took the designs from Ryan Meinerding's design team, and then one of our digital artists here—Won-il Song—created a digital sculpture."

"I designed this to be a seamless forearm piece," Mahan continues. "And after the digital sculpture has been done, and the part has been grown and cleaned up, it matches up to a bicep piece. One of our artists, Chris Swift, is pictured testing it."

Legacy created two versions of the Winter Soldier's arm. "We made one from foam rubber with tracking markers on it for extreme action," Mahan says. "And then there were these arms made of urethane that were metalized and had less action mobility, but for certain shots looked reflective and really great."

MERCS

Christian Cordella
concept illustrations.

Costume Illustrator Christian Cordella: "Along with the Costume Designer, Judianna Markovsky, we went through different versions and ideas to see how the mercenaries could work, and we went from black to gray to distinguish them from Winter Soldier and Captain America. It was all about figuring out how they could become threatening without becoming too unrealistic."

"We did so much research into cargo pants and jackets," Cordella continues. "And gloves, which create a more sinister look in this kind of character, give a sense they can do anything because they're clothed and protected from head to toe. Maybe fingerless is better for shooting, but there are so many interesting thin gloves right now."

WINTER SOLDIER ATTACKS
STORYBOARDS BY PROOF, INC./MONTY GRANITO, DARRIN DENLINGER & CORAL D'ALESSANDRO

The Winter Soldier's surprise attack was initially planned to occur on a drawbridge over the Potomac. Monty Granito, Proof, Inc.'s Previsualization Supervisor, talks about the first sequence Proof, Inc. worked on for the film: "Early on, the focus was to create a quiet moment of exposition, and then have the Winter Soldier surprise us and be everywhere at once. It was important to keep the camera in the car and not see the Winter Soldier to make him appear larger than life. The directors' mantra for this sequence was '70s thriller, grounded. They wanted us to feel claustrophobic and helpless."

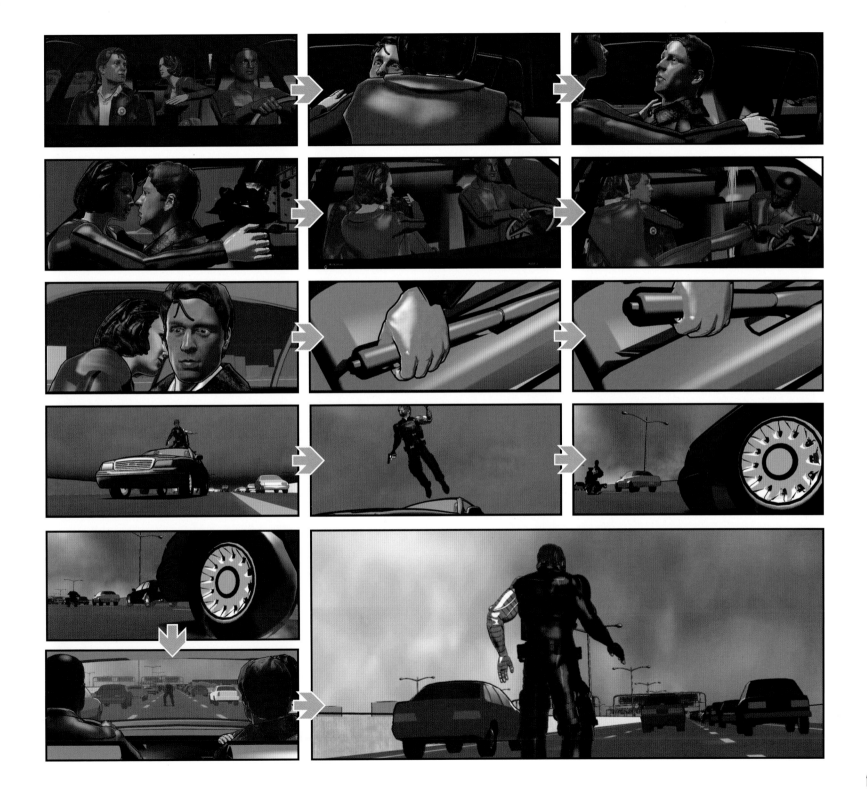

The team worked to highlight the relentlessness and skill of the Winter Soldier, who is fast and powerful and a real threat. "We crafted Winter Soldier's divide-and-conquer strategy and made the drawbridge set based on the location they were going to use," Granito continues. "We created a model of the actual car they were going to use, so we could see if the camera could move around in it and if the characters could pull off the choreography. Originally, the Winter Soldier pulls Sitwell out of the back window, but the real vehicle's back window wasn't big enough for that action."

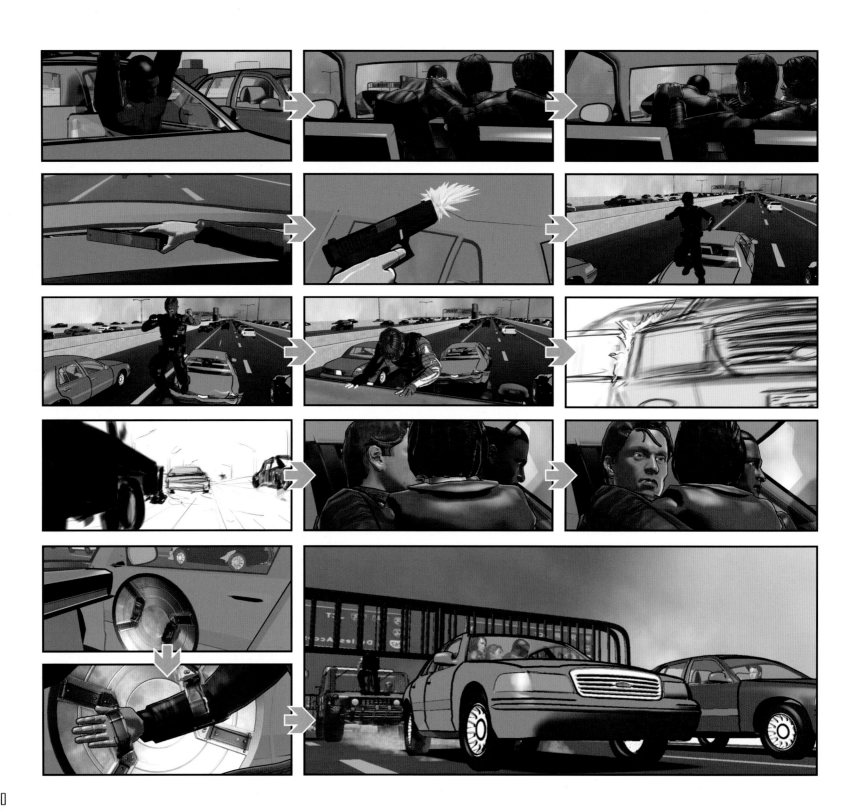

Storyboard Artist Darrin Denlinger revised the sequence after a changing script and location limitations altered the scene. "The Proof previs team had already created a beautifully rendered CG-animated sequence for this massive scene that needed to be extensively altered," Denlinger says. "Usually, I work with a director to create the initial versions of a sequence to hand off to the previs team. In this instance, however, Animatics Editor Coral D'Alessandro and I reconstructed the sequence—culling together as many of the previs shots that I could still use, and generating more based on our locations and timing constraints, in an attempt to retain the magic from the fully animated previs sequence that got everyone excited in the first place."

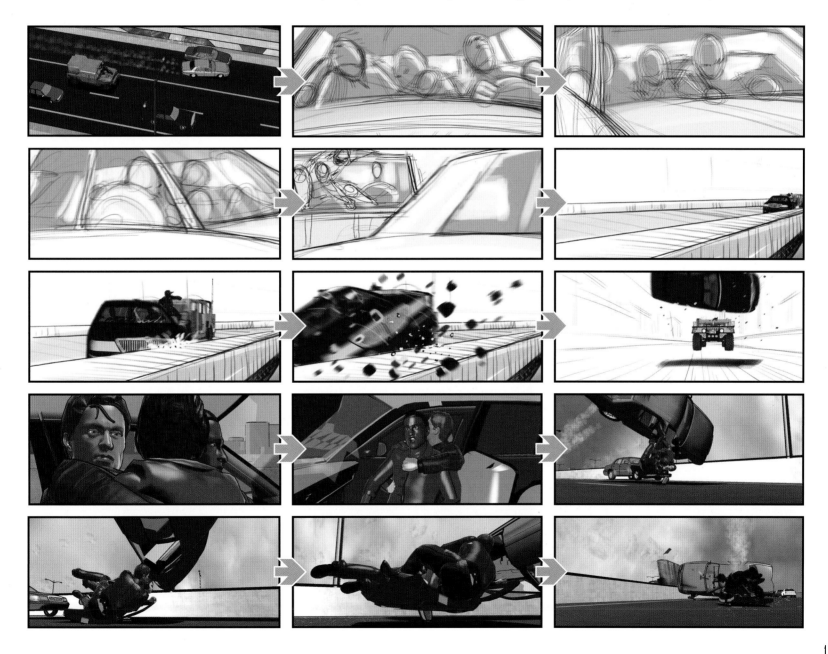

"Cutting the animatic for this scene was a unique challenge because it ultimately became a mix of storyboards, previs, and stunt footage that needed to feel like a cohesive whole," D'Alessandro adds. "Stitching together different pieces of music to create a unifying soundtrack became key to infusing the scene with excitement and maintaining a sense of flow."

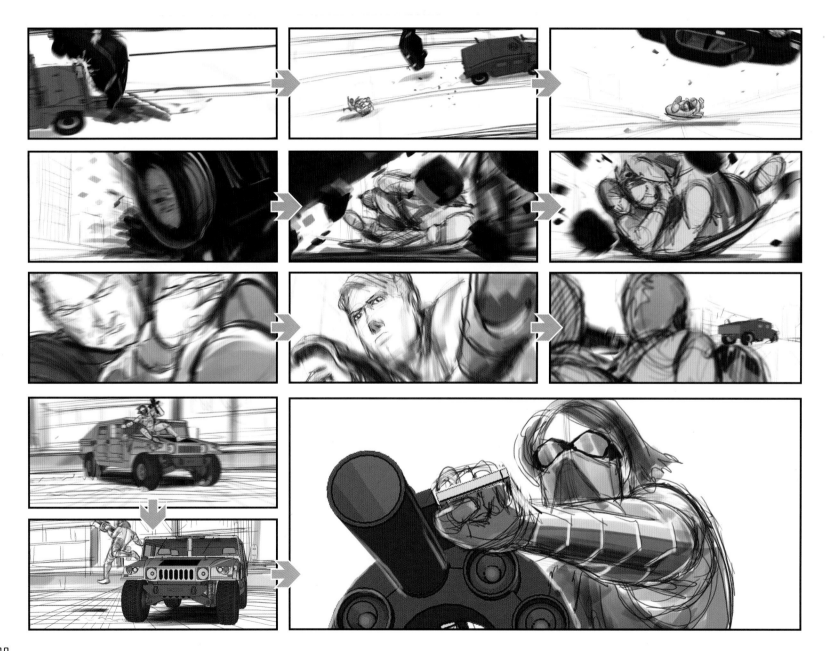

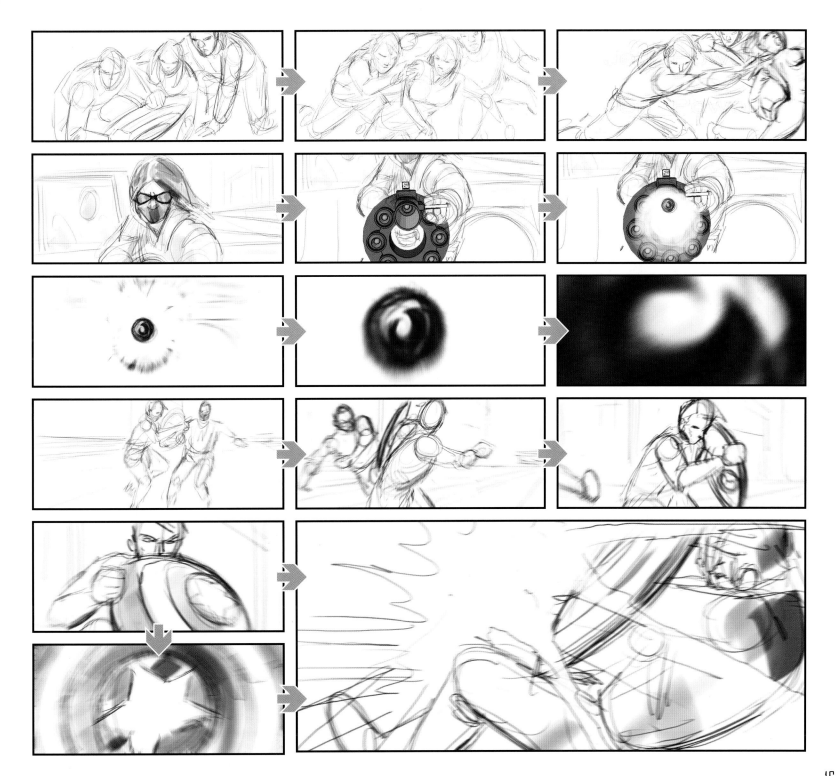

Ryan Meinerding keyframe.

Ryan Meinerding: "One of the reasons we did so many variations on Winter Soldier is he's one of the only characters designed in modern times. Most of the characters we work on don't necessarily have modern roots. They usually have a long story and history and were designed over 50 years ago.

Obviously, Winter Soldier is Bucky, and Bucky has a storied history. But Winter Soldier doesn't necessarily go back that far. One of the things that happens when characters get designed in a modern context is usually they give us touchstones that are easier to translate into film."

Ryan Meinerding keyframe.

World Security Council head Alexander Pierce, portrayed by Robert Redford, is one of the only men to whom Nick Fury listens. But now, Captain America must choose between following his instincts and being a good soldier who obeys his superiors' orders.

"As guys who grew up on '70s thrillers, there is a great symmetry to getting somebody like Robert Redford for this film, especially because of the roots of this movie in *Three Days of the Condor*," Director Joe Russo explains. "From a cultural standpoint,

it's fun—not to mention that he's one of the great actors of all time and the biggest icon that we have in the business."

Director Anthony Russo agrees. "Pierce is a very complicated character, and the great thing about having Robert Redford in that character is when Pierce says it, it's true, because Robert Redford says it. And that was very useful in terms of the storytelling, and the emotional and dramatic dynamics in the film."

Rodney Fuentebella keyframe.

CHAPTER SIX
S.H.I.E.L.D.
DISASSEMBLED

Truth and transparency are timeless. Conspiracies built over decades crumble as the purity of Steve Rogers' moral center eclipses the corruption and compromised ethics that have seeped into the intelligence community with its preemptive strikes, sleeper agents, and undercover operatives.

The man out of time does not, in the end, need to adjust to the modern world. Rather, the modern world must raise its standards to accommodate his simple concepts of justice. And as Captain America reforges the present using ideas formed in years long past, one question remains:

What now?

The Falcon joins Cap in his quest to illuminate secrets in the dark corners of the halls of power.

The two men meet early in the film in an organic and unplanned way, explains Co-producer Nate Moore. "They're both running on the National Mall in D.C. one day. They strike up a conversation. Initially, Steve doesn't know that Sam has a very specialized skill of being able to fly the Exo-7 Falcon, which is the jetpack/wing suit that Sam ends up using in the third act."

Steve Rogers doesn't have many friends in the modern world, but the traits he shares with Sam Wilson transcend eras.

"Sam Wilson comes from the military. They bond right from the beginning, because they were both in similar work," Creative Executive Trinh Tran says.

The two men seamlessly team up on the battlefield—much as Captain America worked with Bucky seventy years ago.

SAM WILSON/FALCON

Concept Artist Josh Nizzi designed the Falcon for the Visual Development team. "We put Nizzi through the paces on this one," Head of Visual Development Ryan Meinerding says. "Falcon was an interesting design challenge, because he is so unrealistic and pure in his comic tradition."

Nizzi abandoned the classic bird-wing look of the comic-book Falcon, instead experimenting with dozens of more realistic options.

"We did a lot of explorations of what his wings would look like," Nizzi explains. "Are they a glider suit? Are they mechanical wings? How bird-like are they? Do they look like wings from an airplane? There were tons of different explorations. Ultimately, what was decided on was a mix of different levels of flexibility in the armature, almost with a sailboat kind of material. And then we added some additional tines in there, but the big reference was sails from sailboats."

Josh Nizzi concept art.

"Where we started was looking for something that was going to make the military wing suits feel cooler and more maneuverable and more fantastical, and at the same time as believable as something you might see in a documentary," Meinerding says. "One of the ways that Joe Russo described it was that he wanted Falcon to feel more maneuverable than Iron Man.

"In terms of where we started from, within the Marvel Universe, Iron Man is the technological bar. We're always trying to find where the character we're working on relates to that bar. And we got the idea that this was a little less sophisticated, but it had a bit more grace than power. When he's up in the air moving, he becomes this incredibly graceful and highly maneuverable character."

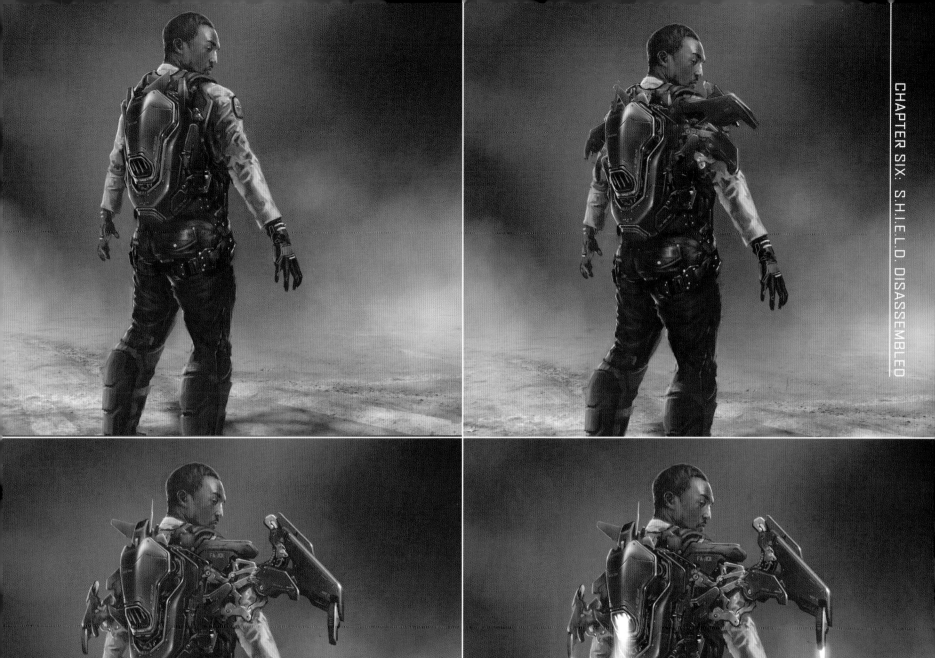

Rodney Fuentebella concept art.

175

"The Falcon's backpack was a really nice piece of construction with a lot of different materials," says Shane Mahan, Physical Suit Effects Supervisor at Legacy Effects. "Ryan's team designed it, and we built it with sculpture, fabrication, and leatherwork. The digital artist was Greg Smith, and the key fabricator was Chris Swift."

Nizzi was present for the final fitting. "It looked supercool," he says. "Some of the fans are going to love it, but some of them are going to wonder why he's not in tights with red feathers like in the comic book."

Producer Kevin Feige explains: "Falcon has been around since the late '60s and—as all Marvel costumes do through the decades—his costume has undergone a transition. Sometimes it's white and low-cut with an open chest and reddish feathers, and other times it's more practical and militaristic. We wanted to do a little bit of both. So you'll see it has its roots in a pararescue team that we're saying Sam Wilson was a part of, but the wings open very much like the classic silhouette of the Falcon."

177

Josh Nizzi
concept art.

178

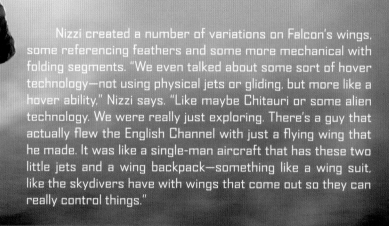

Nizzi created a number of variations on Falcon's wings, some referencing feathers and some more mechanical with folding segments. "We even talked about some sort of hover technology—not using physical jets or gliding, but more like a hover ability," Nizzi says. "Like maybe Chitauri or some alien technology. We were really just exploring. There's a guy that actually flew the English Channel with just a flying wing that he made. It was like a single-man aircraft that has these two little jets and a wing backpack—something like a wing suit, like the skydivers have with wings that come out so they can really control things."

179

"The wings are a mix of different materials, so they look like they could be layered," Nizzi continues. "They needed to be really thin to look like they could collapse into his backpack. The actual armature is very small, and the fabric-like material is stretched over other stuff and has different levels of rigidity."

Josh Nizzi concept art.

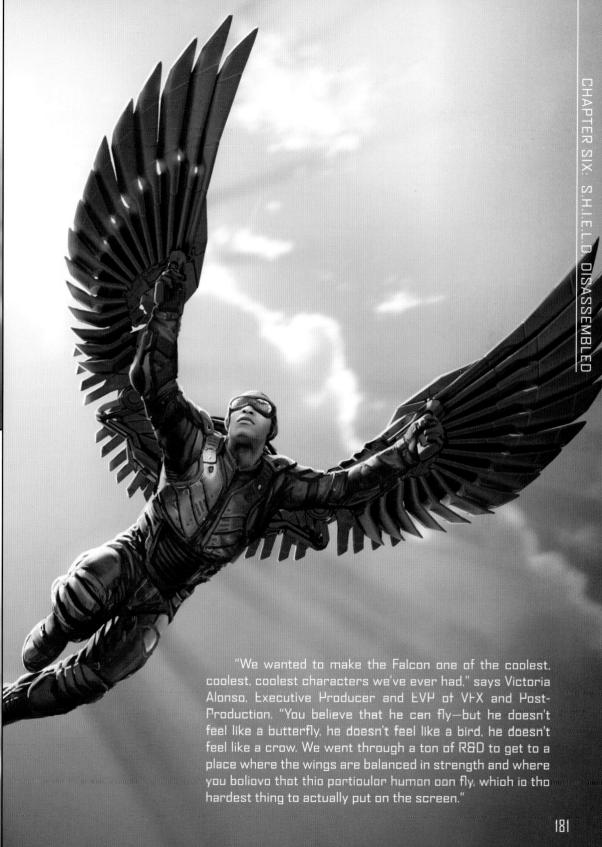

"We wanted to make the Falcon one of the coolest, coolest, coolest characters we've ever had," says Victoria Alonso, Executive Producer and EVP of VFX and Post-Production. "You believe that he can fly—but he doesn't feel like a butterfly, he doesn't feel like a bird, he doesn't feel like a crow. We went through a ton of R&D to get to a place where the wings are balanced in strength and where you believe that this particular human can fly, which is the hardest thing to actually put on the screen."

Concept Artist Andy Park contributed some initial designs to the evolution of the Falcon's wings. "I was also trying to figure out how his guns would work along with the wings," he says. "So I designed it as an attachment to the front of the wings."

Andy Park concept art.

CHAPTER SIX: S.H.I.E.L.D. DISASSEMBLED

Ryan Meinerding concept art.

183

"Falcon's wings are all digital," Trinh Tran says. "Actor Anthony Mackie wore the Legacy Effects backpack, but the wings are all digital. We did build small wings as VFX reference."

Mahan explains how the half-scale reference wing works: "See how it reacts with sunlight? This gives the digital team the lighting reference, whether it is outdoors or on-set lighting. It shows how those wings react. It's part of the reference pass, and makes their job a little easier and more authentic. Part of our job is to help assist Visual Effects. If you actually construct something the physical world can react to, you can sample it instead of making it up."

Legacy Effects also created a full-size mannequin for an early construction of the suit on Mackie's form, with a foam-core facsimile of one wing for size.

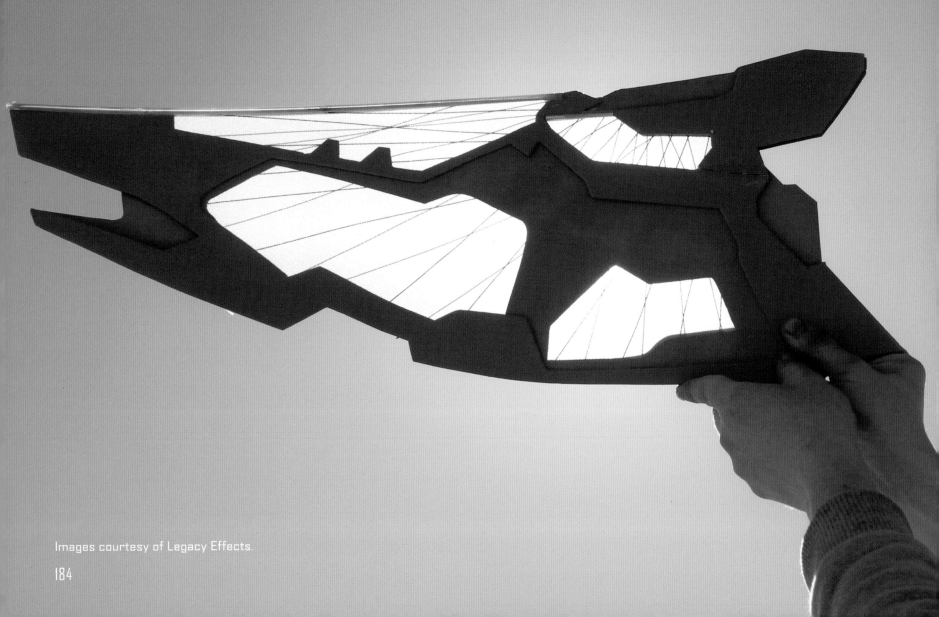

Images courtesy of Legacy Effects.

Josh Nizzi concept art.

186

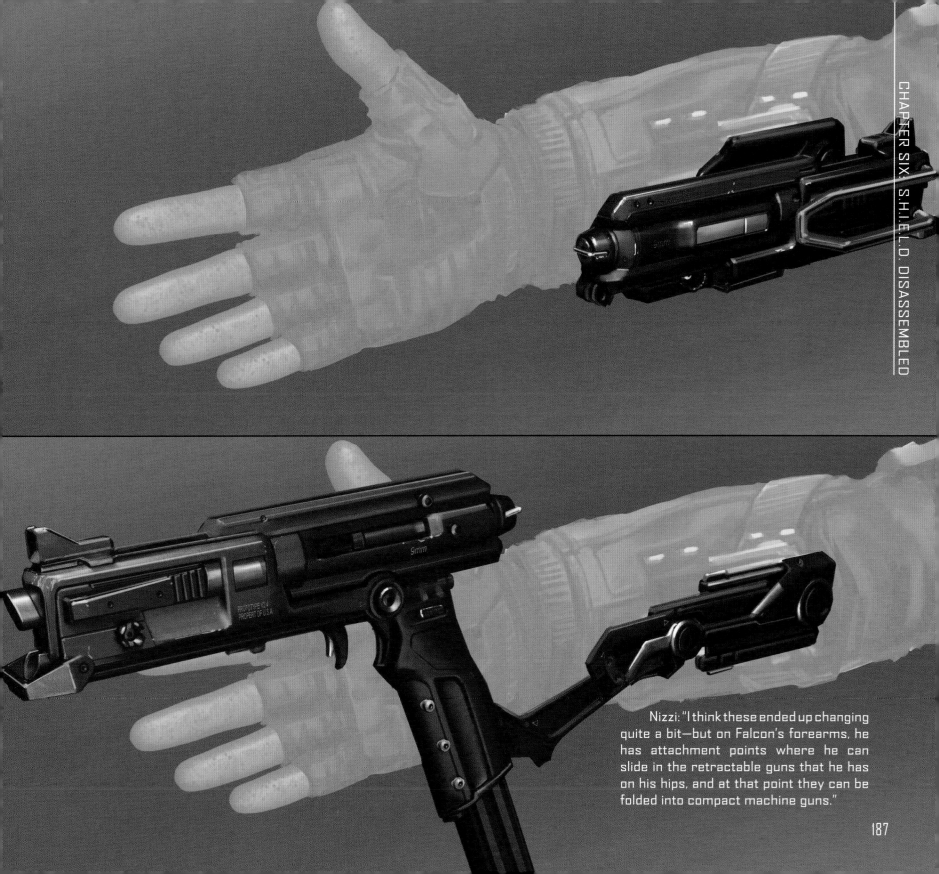

9mm

PROTOTYPE V2.4
PROPERT OF U.S.A

Nizzi: "I think these ended up changing quite a bit—but on Falcon's forearms, he has attachment points where he can slide in the retractable guns that he has on his hips, and at that point they can be folded into compact machine guns."

TRISKELION FINALE
PRE-VISUALIZATION BY MONTY GRANITO

Captain America and Falcon split up, each heading to control rooms on separate Helicarriers. Falcon evades deck guns, but a Quinjet is hot on his tail—so he takes to the skies. Monty Granito—Proof, Inc.'s Previsualization Supervisor—describes what happens next:

"The Quinjet shoots missiles at Falcon, and he gets knocked down. As the Quinjet bursts through the smoke, Falcon shoots at the windshield to distract the pilot, then flies underneath."

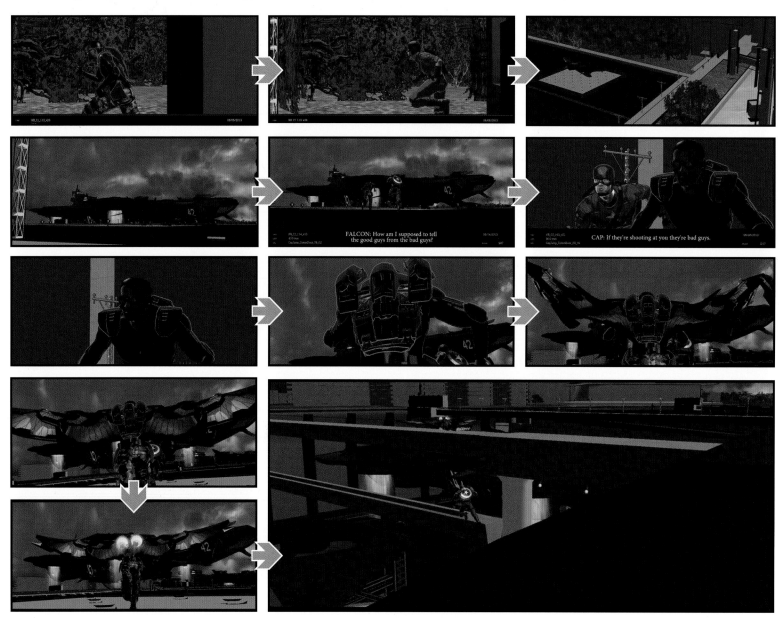

"We received some early sketches of Falcon landing on a Helicarrier," Granito continues. "VFX Supervisor Dan DeLeeuw wanted us to experiment with Falcon's flying and fighting style. I had two artists, Eric Benedict and George Antzoulides, spend some time experimenting and fleshing out a test sequence. Dan, VFX Producer Jen Underdahl, and the directors let us play for a while, and the product of that time became the sequence where Falcon takes on the Helicarriers and Quinjet."

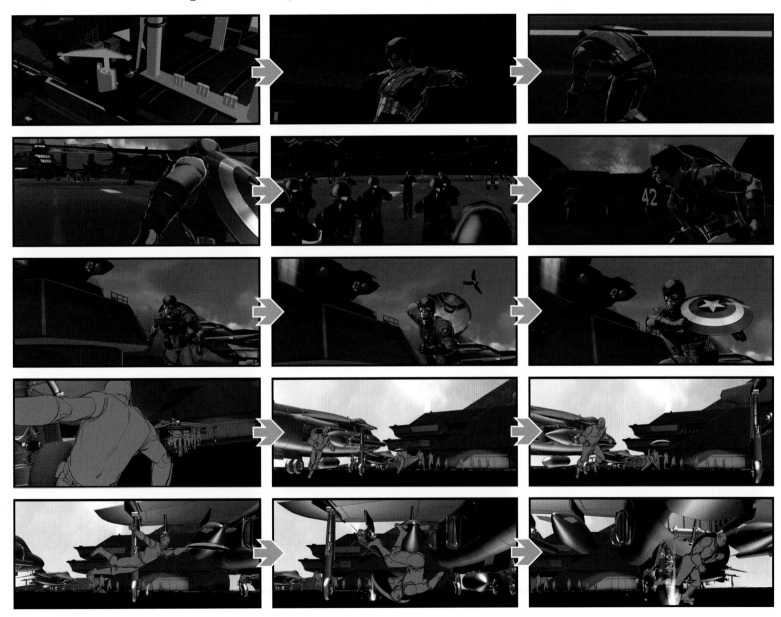

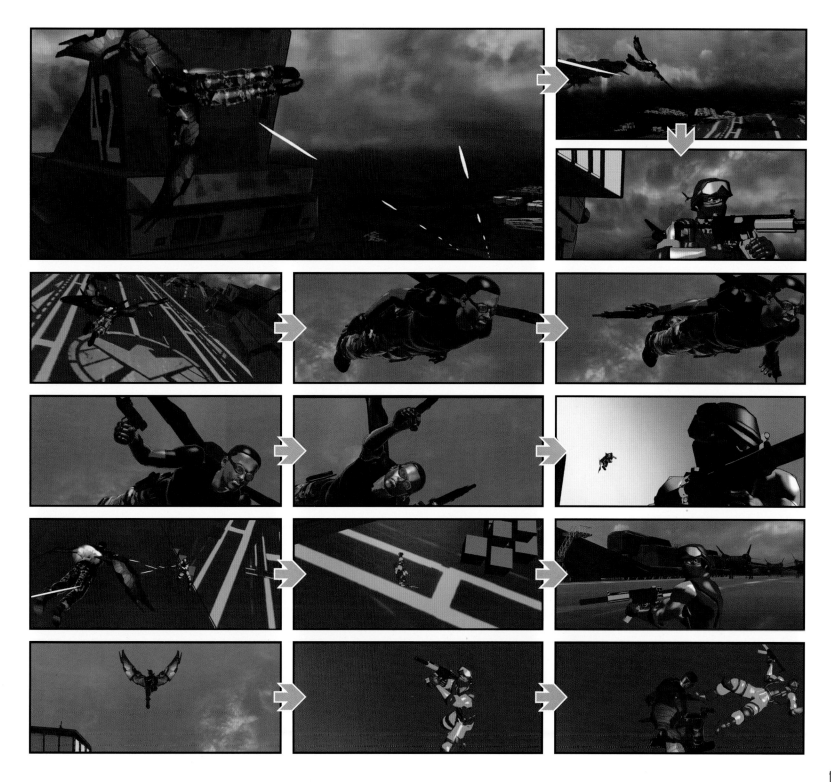

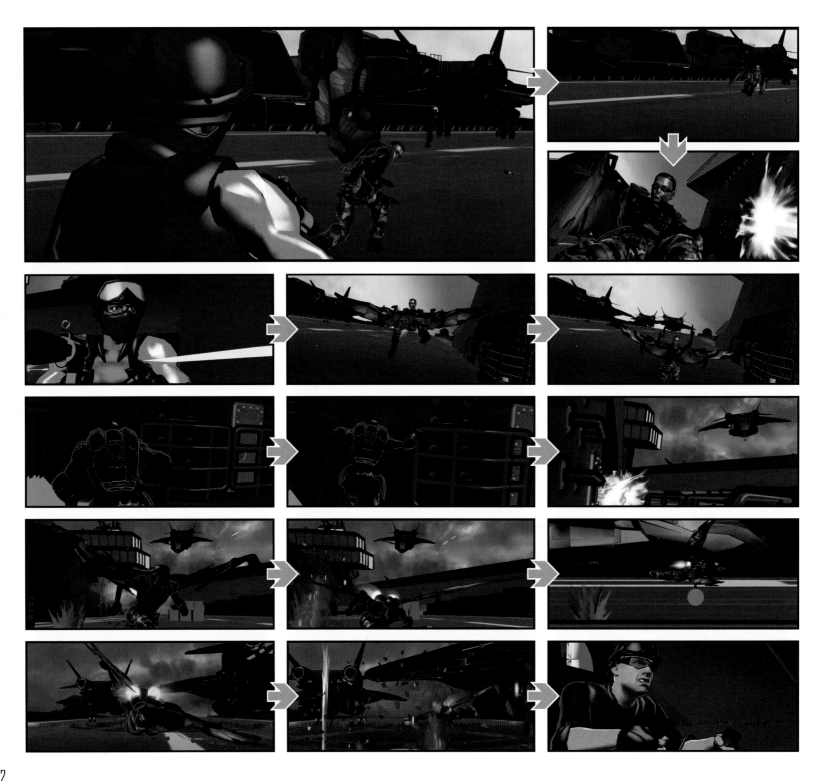

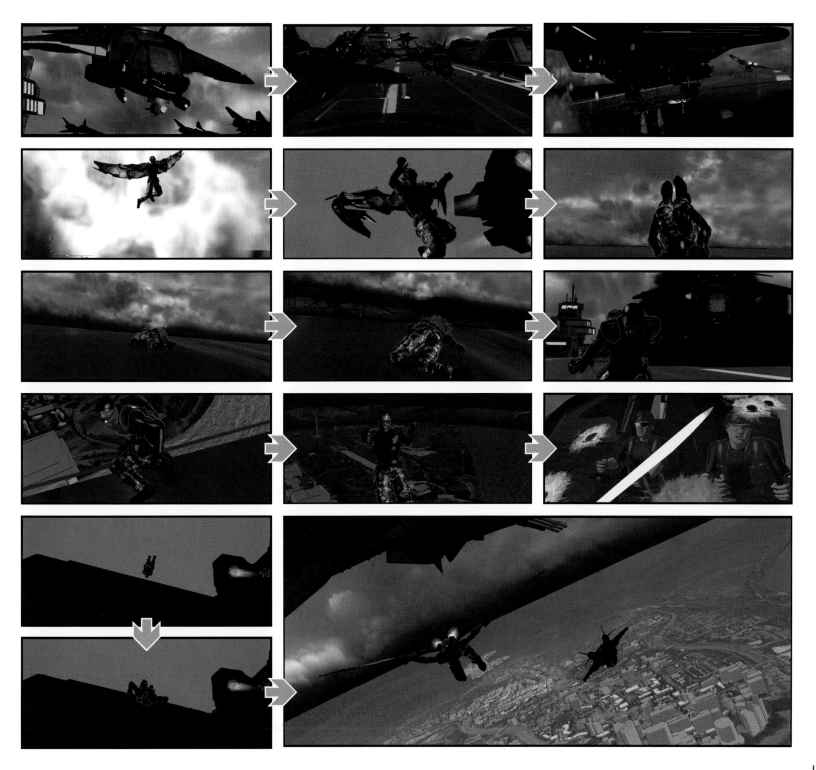

Rodney Fuentebella keyframe.

Concept Artist Rodney Fuentebella: "I wanted to illustrate in the composition how the Falcon is trapped by the Quinjet and its firepower, with the backdrop of the film's epic final battle raging around them. Some key moments in this film are about how Cap and the Falcon are taking on overwhelming forces, and finding a way to triumph and be the heroes we all know and love."

WINTER SOLDIER VS. FALCON
STORYBOARDS BY RICO D'ALESSANDRO

"Even though this scene is only a brief skirmish within the larger battle, it was still important to get it right," Animatics Supervisor and Storyboard Artist Rico D'Alessandro says. "The objective was simple: have Cap and Falcon land on the Helicarrier before Winter Soldier attacks and ultimately throws both men overboard. My challenge was to figure out how all that goes down—making sure the action beats play out in an exciting, dramatic way. For a storyboard artist, these kinds of loose sequences are the most fun to work on because there's a great opportunity to put your own stamp on the movie."

D'Alessandro: "I focused on giving the action beats a frenetic tit-for-tat quality. Winter Soldier immediately takes Cap out of the fight. After Falcon tries to save Cap but is yanked back by Winter Soldier, he reacts by creating distance, which allows him to shoot down from safety. Figuring out how Winter Soldier gets Falcon back down posed another challenge. I love action beats where a character improvises their way out of a situation by utilizing a tool for something other than its intended purpose—so my solution was for Winter Soldier to utilize his grappling hook to pull Falcon to the deck."

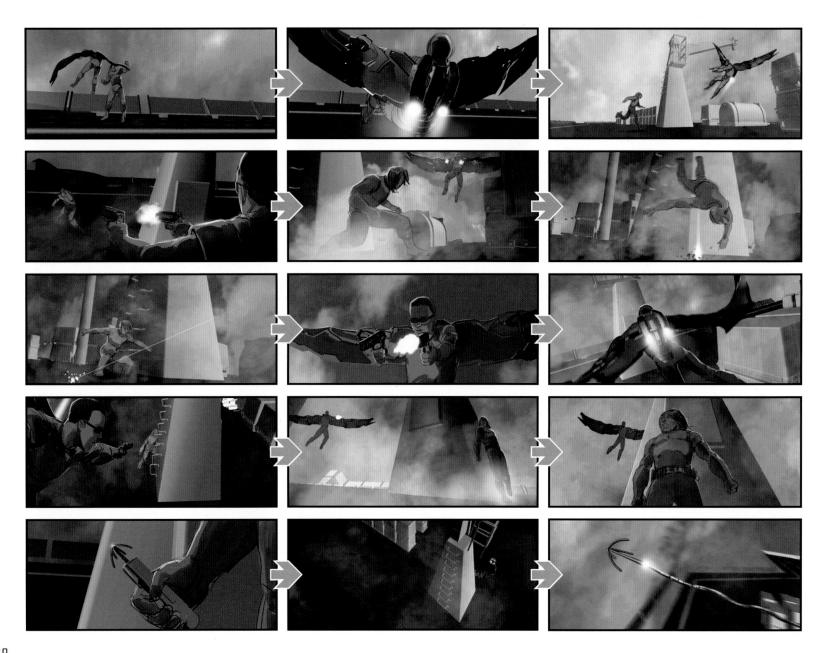

CAPTAIN AMERICA VS. WINTER SOLDIER

STORYBOARDS BY DARRIN DENLINGER

"This whole climactic battle was originally detailed in a gorgeous animatic created by Rico and Coral D'Alessandro," Storyboard Artist Darrin Denlinger says. "As we got closer to filming, it was decided that only portions of the gigantic S.H.I.E.L.D. surveillance bubble environment in which it takes place—beautifully designed by Production Designer Peter Wenham and his Art Department team—would be physically built. The rest would be created by digital set extensions."

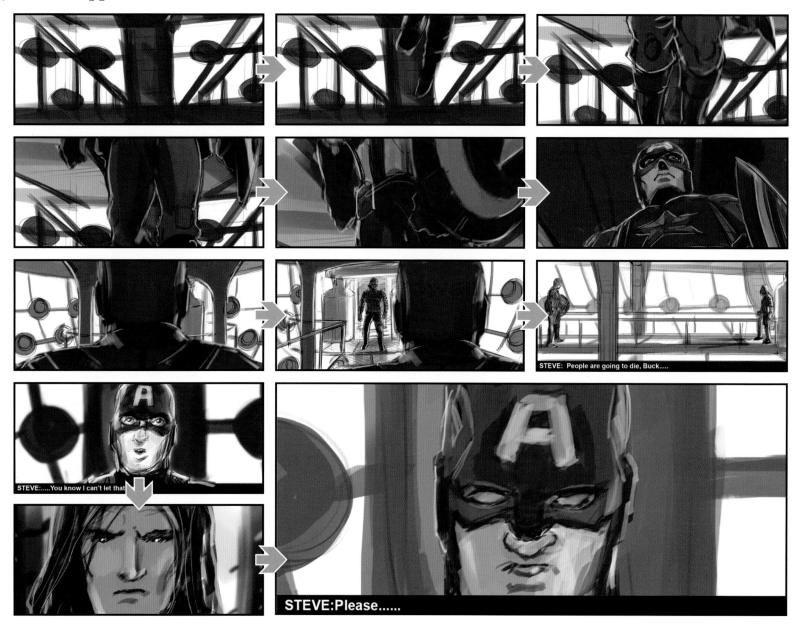

STEVE: People are going to die, Buck.....

STEVE:.....You know I can't let that

STEVE:Please......

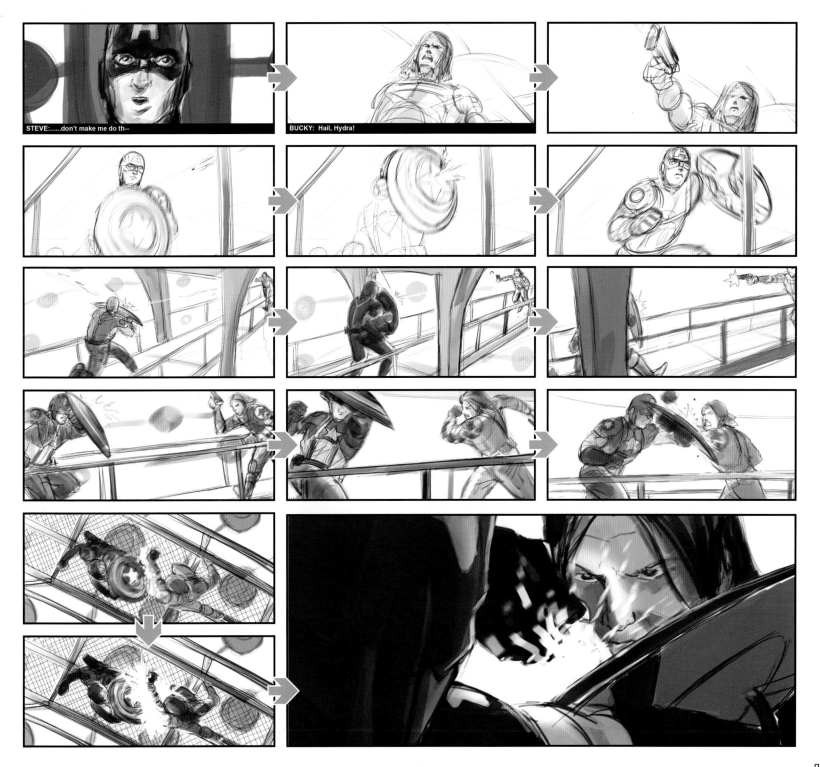

STEVE:......don't make me do th--

BUCKY: Hail, Hydra!

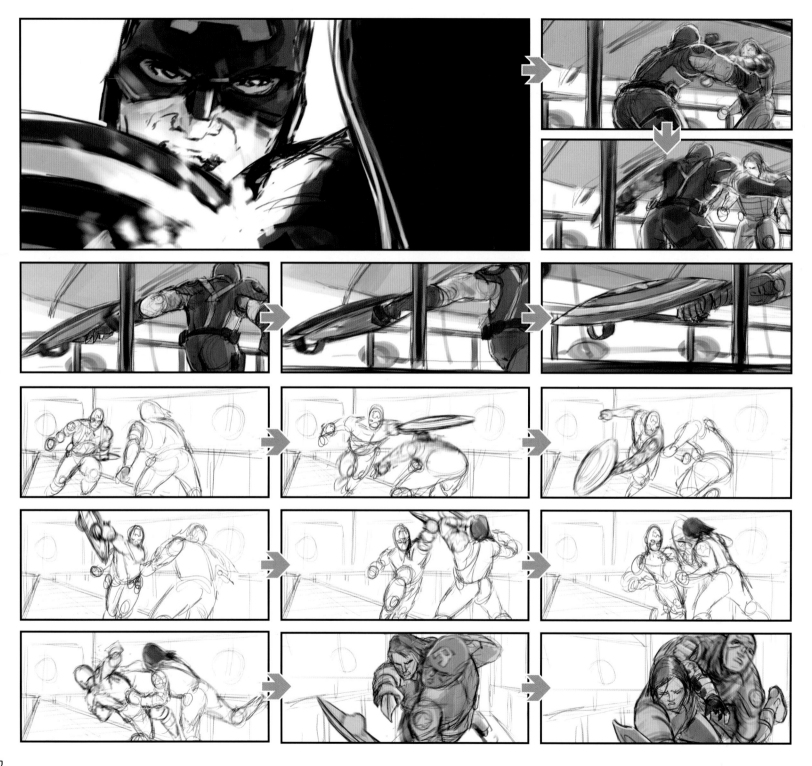

"I was tasked with conforming the animatic battle onto these small sections of actual 'sets,'" Denlinger continues. "When Cap and Winter Soldier tumble over a railing, they often would land on a set piece that physically existed in a different building at the studio. These storyboards provided a blueprint that helped the finished battle appear as though it seamlessly took place in one gigantic environment attached to the underside of the newly designed Helicarrier."

Wenham recalls the difficulties of designing the finale: "There were enormous logistical problems in trying to create this spherical bubble on the scale that it was and to have an action sequence where they are physically fighting on it. There are issues and challenges in having a set that has translucent, safe, spherical shapes that are both concave and convex, and you have to physically fight and work within that environment and light the set, as well."

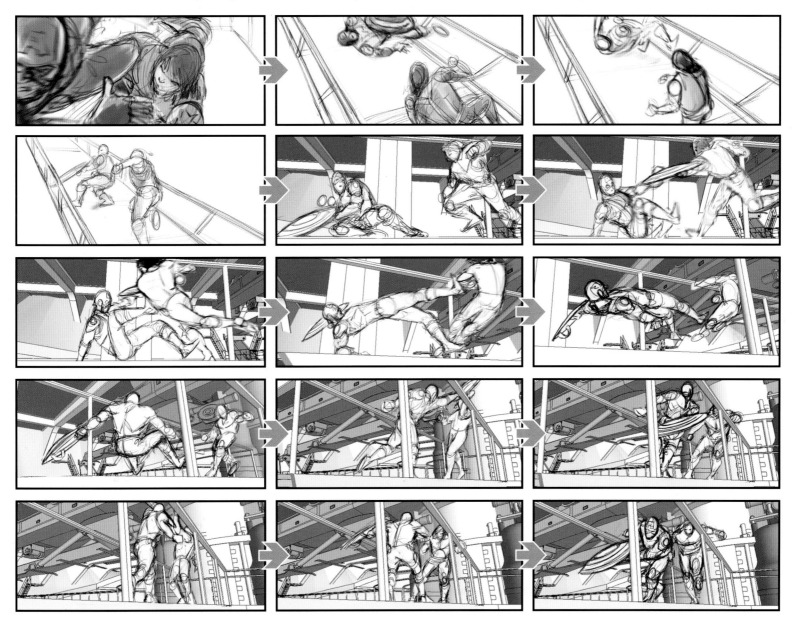

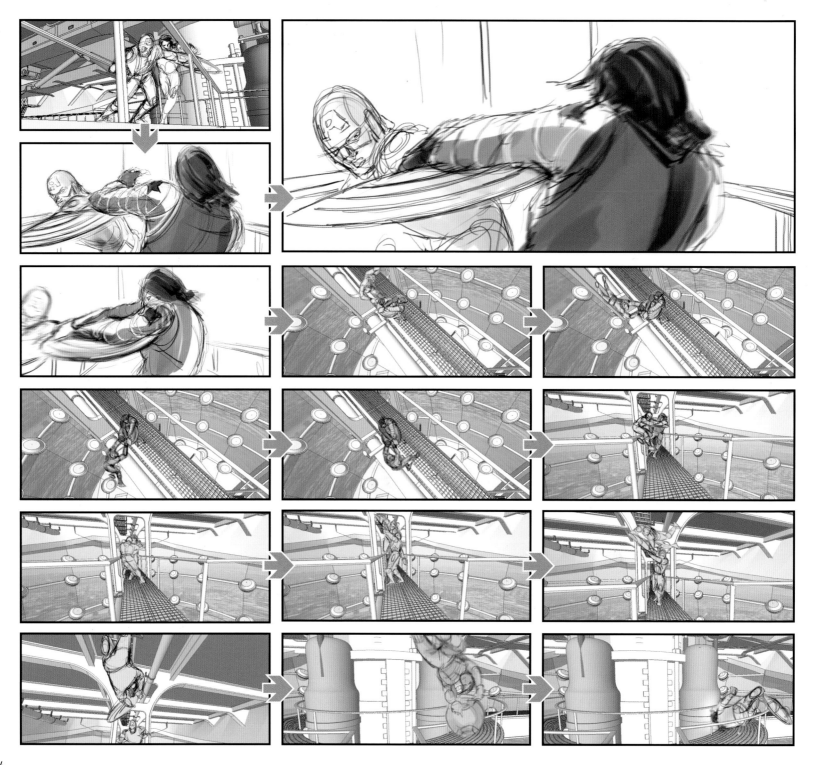

Concept Artist Andrew Kim was asked to illustrate scenes in the finale after Ryan Meinerding saw rough sequential thumbnails Kim had created for a separate task. "It's funny how one small thing leads to something bigger and unexpected," Kim says. "Here, Rumlow is about to finish off Falcon, unaware there's a greater force coming at him in a second."

The Falcon's confrontation with Rumlow became known as the "Forty-First Floor." DeLeeuw explains.

"The set was created with floor tiles that could be racheted up to simulate the Helicarrier pushing through the forty-first floor. The floor's windows were created with broken-glass effects simulations. CG smoke and debris were created to sweeten the effect of the building falling apart."

Andrew Kim keyframe.

Fuentebella found illustrating the epic finale keyframes to be challenging. "I wanted the battle to feel like massive forces are engaging in a life-and-death struggle," he says. "I looked at films of ship battles, various war scenes, and large animals fighting for territorial rights in order to get the feel of this visceral scene of destruction."

The Visual Effects team looked to reference, as well. "We wanted to ground a flying aircraft carrier in reality as much as possible," Visual Effects Supervisor Dan DeLeeuw says. "The guns are tri-barreled. Each barrel fires slightly offset from each other. One of the biggest challenges was to track the damage on each Helicarrier throughout the battle. We used the position of the Helicarriers to determine which one had the best tactical position. As a result, the Helicarrier that is lowest received the most damage. By working from the post-vis, ILM was able to map the damage from every gun. This damage remains consistent through the battle until the Helicarriers ultimately crash."

Rodney Fuentebella concept art.

208

DeLeeuw: "There were multiple versions of each Helicarrier. The pristine versions can be seen lifting off from the Helicarrier bay. The battle-damaged versions show up later in the fight. These versions were designed to show off the damage of every hit and air-to-air collision.

"We tracked the damage on each of the Helicarriers throughout the battle. Each Helicarrier existed as multiple assets—the pristine version, and the versions with augmented damage. We looked at the tactical position of the Helicarriers in the battle and increased the damage appropriately. With each hit, the geometry of the Helicarriers grew. When a Helicarrier crashes, it lands in the Potomac. Water simulations and destruction simulations tear apart the Helicarrier and flood the Helicarrier bay."

Rodney Fuentebella concept art.

Rodney Fuentebella concept art.

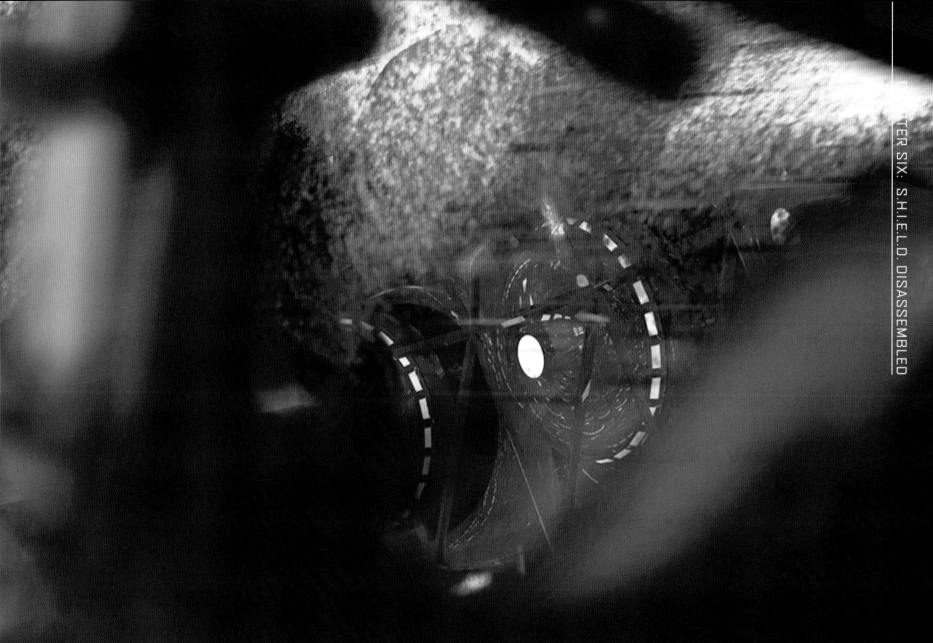

Visual Effects was tasked with rendering ninety percent of the backdrop for the surveillance hub, which existed on three levels as three different sets housed on three different stages.

"If the actors were on the top level of the set, we would create the middle and bottom level in CG," DeLeeuw explains. "Depending on where the action took place, we would create the level above or below the actors. The bottom dome is nestled under the belly of the Helicarrier, and that created the biggest challenge.

"We created a raised set with lights that could shine up through plexiglass. We needed green screen to matte the characters,

so the Grip Department created green baffles around the lights. When viewed from an angle, the baffles hid the lights and created a continuous green screen.

"The dome itself is transparent, which required us to see Washington, D.C., in the distance. Rather than trying to create all of D.C. on the computer, we shot still and moving footage from a helicopter that was tiled together to create a 360-degree cyclorama. This background was then composited behind our actors to give the illusion that they are fighting thousands of feet above the Potomac."

"The idea of this illustration is to show Captain America at the end of the final battle," Fuentebella says. "I wanted it to look like he's alone and on his last breath under the Potomac. Like this is the end for Cap—the battle is won, but with a heavy cost."

DeLeeuw describes shooting the scene: "We used a combination of digital doubles and live action to complete the shots of Cap falling in the water. For close-ups, we dropped Chris Evans into a water tank. A solitary figure drops into camera with a burning Helicarrier in the background. A digital double drops toward camera. The CG surface water creates a distorted lens for the audience to view the dying Helicarrier. Through this distorted lens, the explosion on the Helicarrier almost becomes beautiful. Effects simulations were used on the fire and smoke of the Helicarrier."

Rodney Fuentebella keyframe.

214

CHAPTER SEVEN
MARKETING CAPTAIN AMERICA: THE WINTER SOLDIER

Ryan Meinerding keyframe.

Marvel Studios introduces its upcoming movies to fans at Comic-Con International in San Diego every summer, and Marvel Studios Head of Visual Development Ryan Meinerding enjoys his chance to create an annual giveaway poster.

"Every year, we try to do something that hits the core of what we think is great about each project we're working on," Meinerding says. "To me, that's one of the cooler parts about Marvel. The comics started with art, there is still a love for concept art and art in general at the studio, and Marvel is really willing to let that art get out into the world and be representative of the movies."

Meinerding's poster for *Captain America: The Winter Soldier* started as a tight shot of two portraits leaning into each other but evolved into a scene with more background and reaction.

"I really wanted to capture the personal, one-to-one struggle between the hero and his old friend," Meinerding says. "I set it against the huge battle of the finale—touchstones that are easier to translate into film."

Captain America's shield was used on some theatrical posters. "Since Captain America is in the stealth costume in some scenes, my idea was that the shield has actually become muted, as well, with a new paint covering," Meinerding says. "But there are still places where that paint chips away and you can see the red underneath. Captain America is a symbol, and color on symbols add or subtracts from his statement narrative."

APRIL 2014
WWW.FB.COM/CAPTAINAMERICAMOVIE

Limited-edition collectible poster by Ryan Meinerding, San Diego Comic-Con 2013.

First theatrical teaser poster.

Theatrical one-sheet.

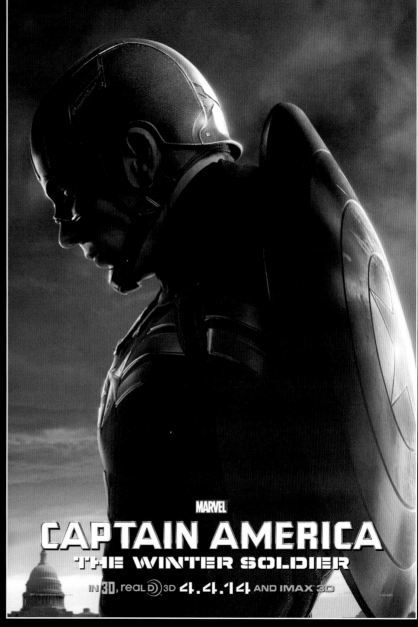

Individual character posters.

Ryan Meinerding keyframe.

222

Working on the Marvel Cinematic Universe is a true gift. Of course there is the obvious—getting to spend every day drawing and working on characters and stories that I love—but the gift Marvel has to offer lies deeper than that.

Most projects in the film industry consist of a four-month gig, and then an artist like me has to find work somewhere else. At Marvel, however, I've been allowed the chance to truly invest in characters across multiple films, and watch them grow and change in ways that could never happen in a single film. In Cap's case, we've seen him sacrifice himself for his country only to wake 70 years later to find that he no longer recognizes much of what he "died" for. Since my job consists of developing designs for characters that achieve the needs of the story and accomplish the director's vision, I've worked on making Cap's journey visual. It's a dream come true to design a character's costume in two periods separated by 70 years and an emotional journey that's even further distancing.

That's what is so amazing about the MCU. It is constantly redefining and refining its characters in such profound ways that it requires solid design directions in order for the costumes and moments to reflect the character's journey. The touchstones of design for Cap started with nostalgic innocence coupled with super-soldier, and have developed into not only a super hero, but also a real leader. Within the pages of this book, you have gotten a taste of the next stage of Cap's adventure.

Furthermore, the Russo brothers' reinvention of Captain America for The Winter Soldier was an extraordinary journey to be a part of. They had a distinct vision of where they wanted to take the character, so the designs of each of Cap's costumes were exercises in joy for me. They wanted to take the super-soldier costume from the comics and turn it into a stealth costume, representing Steve's willingness to do black-ops missions. They were looking to show him becoming part of the complicated modern world of espionage and not enjoying it.

For me, returning to the nostalgia of WWII for the Smithsonian exhibition was honestly one of my favorite projects I've ever done for Marvel. Not only did I get to paint two huge murals, but they were also used with such precision in the story that it makes the hard work doubly rewarding.

I hope the touchstones of design laid out by the Russos are evident on every page of this book, as they are evident in every second of the film.

Thank you, Kevin, Joe, and Anthony, for adding yet another brilliant chapter to Cap's journey within the Marvel Cinematic Universe.

Ryan Meinerding
2014

Directors **Anthony and Joe Russo** are perhaps best-known for their work on the critically acclaimed television shows *Arrested Development*, *Community*, and *Happy Endings*. They directed the pilots to all three shows, as well as many of the series' signature episodes. Born a year apart in Cleveland, Ohio, the Russo Brothers used credit cards and student loans to finance their first film *Pieces*, an experimental comedy shot with the help of family and friends. The film screened at both the Slamdance and American Film Institute festivals in 1997, earning Joe a Best Actor award at the latter. The Slamdance screening caught the attention of filmmaker Steven Soderbergh, who along with his producing partner George Clooney, offered to produce the brothers' second film, the crime comedy *Welcome to Collinwood*. Kevin Reilly was rebuilding the FX Network when he first saw *Welcome to Collinwood*, and he asked the pair to direct the pilot for his new flagship comedy, *Lucky*. Among the pilot's fans was Imagine Entertainment co-founder Ron Howard, who, along with writer Mitch Hurwitz, was looking to take the well-worn situation comedy in a new direction. They sought out the Russos to direct the pilot to *Arrested Development*. The brothers shot the show on HD cameras, minimizing the need for complex lighting and crews, and created the distinctive visual style that was so popular with the show's fan base. They won an Emmy for their direction. In 2008, the brothers directed the pilot to *Community*, and in 2009, the pilot to *Happy Endings*. They partnered with Dan Harmon and David Caspe as Executive Producers and spent the next three years working simultaneously on both shows. Over the last decade, the Russos have directed 12 television pilots, 10 of which have gone to series.

Over the past decade, Producer and Marvel Studios President **Kevin Feige** has played an instrumental role in a string of blockbuster feature films adapted from the pages of Marvel comic books. In his current role as Producer and President of Marvel Studios, Feige oversees all creative aspects of the company's feature film and home entertainment activities. In addition to producing *Captain America: The Winter Soldier*, he is currently producing *Guardians of the Galaxy*, *Avengers: Age of Ultron*, and *Ant-Man*. His previous producing credits for Marvel include *Iron Man 3*, which became the second-largest box office debut in Hollywood history behind the critically acclaimed *Marvel's The Avengers*, which Kevin also produced along with *Thor: The Dark World*, *Thor*, *Captain America: The First Avenger*, *Iron Man 2*, and *Iron Man*.

Executive Producer and Marvel Studios Co-President **Louis D'Esposito** served as Executive Producer on the blockbuster hits *Iron Man*, *Iron Man 2*, *Thor*, *Captain America: The First Avenger*, *Marvel's The Avengers*, *Iron Man 3*, and most recently *Thor: The Dark World*. He is also currently working on *Guardians of the Galaxy* as well as working with Marvel Studios' President Kevin Feige to build the future Marvel slate. As Co-President of the studio and Executive Producer on all Marvel films, D'Esposito balances running the studio to overseeing each film from their development stage to distribution. Beyond his role as Co-President of Marvel Studios, D'Esposito also directs unique filmed projects for the studio including his one-shot titled *Agent Carter* starring Hayley Atwell, and the short film titled *Item 47*. The project was released as an added feature on *Marvel's The Avengers* Blu-ray disc. D'Esposito began his tenure at Marvel Studios in 2006. Prior to Marvel, D'Esposito's executive producing credits include the 2006 hit film *The Pursuit of Happyness* starring Will Smith, *Zathura: A Space Adventure* and the 2003 hit *S.W.A.T.* starring Samuel L. Jackson and Colin Farrell.

Ryan Meinerding keyframe.

Executive Producer **Victoria Alonso** is currently executive producing *Avengers: Age of Ultron* and *Guardians of the Galaxy* for Marvel Studios, where she serves as Executive Vice President of Visual Effects and Post Production. She executive produced *Captain America: The Winter Soldier*, *Thor: The Dark World*, *Iron Man 3*, as well as *Marvel's The Avengers*. She also co-produced *Iron Man* and *Iron Man 2* with director Jon Favreau, *Thor*, and *Captain America: The First Avenger*. Alonso's career began at the nascency of the visual effects industry, when she served as a commercial VFX producer. From there, she VFX-produced numerous feature films, working with such directors as Ridley Scott (*Kingdom of Heaven*), Tim Burton (*Big Fish*) and Andrew Adamson (*Shrek*), to name a few.

Executive Producer **Michael Grillo** started his career in production as a DGA trainee on *Young Frankenstein* and *The Towering Inferno*. He became the second assistant director on *Fun with Dick and Jane*, *New York, New York* with Martin Scorsese and *Deerhunter*, which won the Best Picture Oscar that year. He moved up to first assistant director on numerous productions, then started his long collaboration with director Lawrence Kasdan as his first assistant director on *Body Heat* and *The Big Chill*. With Mr. Kasdan and Mr. Charles Okun, he executive produced *Silverado*, *I Love You To Death*, and *Wyatt Earp*, was co-producer on *Cross My Heart*, and produced *Grand Canyon* and *The Accidental Tourist*, for which he received an Academy Award nomination for Best Picture. Later, he produced *Defending Your Life*, *The Trigger Effect*, and executive produced *The Green Hornet*. He was executive producer on DreamWorks' first feature film, *The Peacemaker*, and served as DreamWorks head of feature film production management from 1996 thru 2005. He executive produced *The Amazing Spider-Man* and is currently prepping *Ant Man*. Mr. Grillo has received two DGA Awards for Best Picture as assistant director and is a member of the Academy of Motion Pictures Arts and Sciences and the Directors Guild of America.

Co-Producer **Nate Moore** began his career at Marvel Studios in 2010 working primarily on long lead development and running the Marvel Writer's Program. *Captain America: The Winter Soldier* is the first Marvel feature film that Moore has overseen. Moore got his start in the film industry working at Columbia Pictures and Exclusive Media, working on numerous feature films. An avid Marvel Comics fan, he is excited to help bring to life the expanding world of Captain America.

Production Designer **Peter Wenham** began his career at the BBC in 1987, after studying interior design and architecture at De Montfort University. He became an Art Director for television programs including *Poirot*, at the UK's Independent Television (ITV) and London Weekend Television (LWT). He then ventured into film and television movies and received Emmy Award Nominations for Outstanding Art Direction for a Miniseries, Movie, or Special for both *Hornblower: Mutiny* and *Hornblower: Duty*. Wenham's success in television and television movies led to working in UK feature films as a Supervising Art Director, on films including *The Bourne Supremacy*, *Kinky Boots*, *The Queen*, which was nominated for an ADG Award for Excellence in Production Design, and *Blood Diamond*. His work on *The Bourne Supremacy* led to becoming the Production Designer for *The Bourne Ultimatum*, which he was nominated for an ADG Award for Excellence in Production Design. After Bourne, Wenham production designed U.S. films such as *Battle Los Angeles*, *Fast Five*, *21 Jump Street*, and *Now You See Me*. Wenham is currently working with Director Chris Columbus on *Pixels* starring Adam Sandler.

Costume Designer **Judianna Makovsky** is a three-time Academy Award nominee whose designs for *Seabiscuit*, *Harry Potter and the Sorcerer's Stone*, and *Pleasantville* have been recognized with Oscar nominations as well as being honored by her peers with Costume Designers Guild Awards for the latter two films. She also received a BAFTA nomination for *Harry Potter and the Sorcerer's Stone*. Most recently, Makovsky designed the costumes for *The Hunger Games* and *The Last Airbender*, and the recently completed *Look of Love*. Some of her other credits include *Cirque du Freak*, *X-Men: The Last Stand*, both *National Treasure* films, *The Legend of Bagger Vance*, *Practical Magic*, *Lolita*, *Mr. Brooks*, *A Little Princess*, *The Quick and the Dead*, *The Devil's Advocate*, *White Squall*, and *Reversal of Fortune*, and *Great Expectations*. Makovsky has a BFA from The School of the Art Institute of Chicago, and also attended The Goodman School of Drama as well as the MFA program at Yale University School of Drama.

Director of Photography **Trent Opaloch** started working behind a camera in his early teen years helping his stepfather, a wildlife cameraman on nature documentaries. After film school Opaloch began his career shooting short films, music videos, and commercials before filming Neill Blomkamps' Oscar nominated *District 9*. Trent's work on *District 9* was nominated for Best Cinematography at the 2010 BAFTA Film Awards as well as the CSC and OFCS awards. In addition to Marvel's *Captain America: The Winter Soldier*, Opaloch's feature film credits include Blomkamps' *Elysium* starring Matt Damon and Jodie Foster, and *Chappie* starring Hugh Jackman and Sigourney Weaver.

Head of Visual Development **Ryan Meinerding** has only been active as a freelance concept artist and illustrator in the film business since 2005, but his work is already drawing the kind of raves reserved for veterans of the industry. After earning a degree in industrial design from Notre Dame, he transitioned to Hollywood and worked on *Outlander*. Subsequent to *Iron Man*, he worked on *Transformers: Revenge of the Fallen* and illustrated costumes on *Watchmen*. While working on Iron Man 2, Meinerding contributed the design for the new Iron Man armor in the comic-book series *Invincible Iron Man*, continuing to cement the strong bonds between Marvel Studios and Marvel Comics. He was part of the *Iron Man* crew nominated for the 2009 Art Directors Guild Excellence in Production Design Award for Fantasy Films; was one of the main concept designers for *Thor*; and served as Visual Development Co-Supervisor on *Captain America: The First Avenger* and *Marvel's The Avengers*, and Head of Visual Development on *Iron Man 3*, *Captain America: The Winter Soldier*, and *Avengers: Age of Ultron*.

Physical Suit Effects Supervisor **Shane Mahan** worked with Stan Winston for over two decades, so it was only natural that—along with colleagues Lindsay MacGowan, Alan Scott, and John Rosengrant—he founded his own FX company. Since opening its doors in 2008, Legacy Effects has been involved with a series of high-profile films, including involvement in Marvel Studios Phase One of the Marvel Cinematic Universe. Co-owner and FX Supervisor Shane Mahan has played an important role in bringing practical effects to life in films including *Iron Man*, *Iron Man 2*, *Thor*, *Marvel's The Avengers*, *Iron Man 3*, and *Pacific Rim*. Concurrently, the Legacy Effects studio has been involved in a wide range of film productions such as *Avatar*, *Snow White & The Huntsman*, *The Muppets*, *Life of Pi*, *The Bourne Legacy*, *Twilight: Breaking Dawn* and the upcoming films *Robocop*, *Seventh Son* and *Marvel's Captain America: The Winter Soldier*.

Property Master **Russell Bobbitt's** resume includes all three of Marvel's *Iron Man* films, *Thor*, and *Captain America: The Winter Soldier*, as well as *Oz: The Great and Powerful*, *The Hangover*, *The Hangover Part II*, and J.J. Abrams' *Star Trek*. Tasked with the design, manufacturing, and acquisition of film props, as well as the establishment of prop continuity from scene to scene, Bobbitt has been developing the physical reality of iconic movies for 30 years. He has twice won Hamilton's prestigious "Behind the Camera" Award for Best Property Master. He has also won two Telly Awards for directing. He resides in Los Angeles with his wife, Tracy, and daughter Jordan.

Visual Effects Supervisor **Dan DeLeeuw** was the overall VFX supervisor for Marvel's *Captain America: The Winter Soldier*. Dan grew up in Southern California and started creating effects at an early age. He would spend his summer vacations building miniatures that would be destroyed in spectacular fashion on the 4th of July. After college, DeLeeuw started working at Dream Quest Images as the second employee in their digital division. He was Digital Supervisor on *Crimson Tide*, *The Rock*, and *Reign of Fire*. He branched into character animation, and worked at Rhythm and Hues VFX Supervising *Night at the Museum*, which made it to the Academy VFX Bakeoff. Dan joined the Marvel team when he supervised second unit on *Iron Man 3*.

Visual Effects Producer **Jen Underdahl's** experience in film and television spans 11 years and includes some of Hollywood's most respected films. She has been with Marvel for nearly four years and during that time has served as a VFX Executive on the *The Avengers*, Visual Effects Producer on Marvel One-Shot: *Item 47*, and VFX Production Manager on the first installment of Captain America, The First Avenger. Prior to working at Marvel she worked freelance on such projects as Gore Verbinski's *Pirates of the Caribbean: At World's End*, the Wachowski's *Speed Racer*, Chris Columbus' *Percy Jackson and the Lightning Thief*, Clint Eastwood's WWII duo-film project, *Flags of our Fathers* and *Letters from Iwo Jima*. Before making the move into digital effects, Jen began her career in the model shop, building practical miniatures and props for film and television. She has been credited on such effects-heavy films as Jon Favreau's *Zathura: A Space Adventure*, Rob Cohen's *Stealth* and Roland Emmerich's *The Day After Tomorrow*.

Concept Artist **Rodney Fuentebella** has degrees in design from UCLA and Product Design from the Art Center College of Design. Born in the Philippines and raised in San Francisco, he has worked on various projects for Electronic Arts, Atari, Rhythm and Hues, Dreamworks Animation, and WIRED magazine, as well as various other entertainment and commercial projects. In film, he worked as a concept artist at Rhythm and Hues before joining the Visual Development team at Marvel Studios. Rodney has created key-art illustrations and character designs for *Captain America: The First Avenger*, *Marvel's The Avengers*, *Iron Man 3*, and upcoming Marvel Studios films.

Concept Artist **Andy Park** began his career illustrating comic books for about a decade on titles such as *Tomb Raider*, *Excalibur*, and *Uncanny X-Men* for companies like Marvel, DC, and Image Comics. In 2004, he began working as a concept artist in video games and television. He was one of the leading artists creating the worlds and characters of the award-winning *God of War* franchise for Sony Computer Entertainment of America. Park has since joined the team at Marvel Studios as a visual development illustrator, designing characters and keyframes for *Marvel's The Avengers*, *Captain America: The First Avenger*, *Iron Man 3*, and the upcoming *Guardians of the Galaxy*, *Captain America: The Winter Soldier*, and *The Avengers: Age of Ultron*.

Concept Artist **Josh Nizzi** graduated from the University of Illinois with a degree in Graphic Design. He spent the next nine years working in video games as an art director, concept artist, modeler, and animator on games like *Red Faction I* and *2*, *The Punisher*, *MechAssault 2*, and *Fracture*. Since then, Josh has been an illustrator for feature films such as *Transformers 2*, *3*, and *4*, *The Amazing Spider-Man*, *Marvel's The Avengers*, *The Avengers: Age of Ultron*, *Django Unchained*, and *The Wolverine*. He continues to work on video game projects as well as venturing into toys, comics, and television.

Storyboard Artist **Darrin Denlinger** taught himself to draw by copying Marvel Comics covers all through middle school. After watching *Superman: The Movie* and *Alien* as a teenager, the twin passions of art and cinema sent him on a twisty journey studying film production at SDSU and spending years learning the inner workings of Hollywood in a variety of positions at Universal Studios and Sony Pictures. When dear friend George Huang offered him a chance to do storyboards on his teen comedy *Trojan War*, Darrin had found his calling. Darrin has contributed to a wide variety of films, from *Pirates of the Caribbean* to *Bridesmaids*. Considering his childhood fixation with comic book covers, Darrin's current tenure on Marvel films such as *The Incredible Hulk*, *Thor*, *Captain America: The First Avenger*, *Marvel's The Avengers*, and *Iron Man 3* has been a dream come true. Darrin lives in Los Angeles with the love of his life, Mari, and two amazing sons, Aidan and Nate. He is currently finishing up work on *The Avengers: Age of Ultron*.

Storyboard Artist **Richard Bennett Lamas** is Uruguayan by birth but moved to New York to start a career in the comic book field. For ten years, he worked there for several companies including Marvel and Image before relocating to enroll at the Art Center College of Design in Pasadena. He studied illustration there and since graduation, he's been working in the motion picture industry. Among some of the films he collaborated on are *AVP*, *Zodiac*, *The Curious Case of Benjamin Button*, *The Social Network*, *Mission: Impossible-Ghost Protocol*, *Oblivion*, and *Star Trek*. More recently he worked on *Tomorrowland*, *Marvel's The Avengers*, and *Captain America: The Winter Soldier*.

Storyboard Artist and Animatics Supervisor **Federico D'Alessandro** has made a name for himself as one of the top storyboard artists in Hollywood and a key creative force behind a multitude of blockbuster films. Cutting his teeth on large-scale productions like *I Am Legend*, *Where the Wild Things Are*, and *The Chronicles of Narnia* series, he became known for his dynamic and immersive animatics that blend the line between storyboards and previs. In 2009, he brought this animatics process to Marvel Studios and became one of their most trusted collaborators, playing an important role in films such as *Thor*, *Captain America: The First Avenger*, *Marvel's The Avengers*, *Iron Man 3*, *Thor: The Dark World*, as well as the upcoming *Avengers 2: Age of Ultron*, and *Ant-Man*.

Proof, Inc. Previsualization Supervisor **Monty Granito** has been a mainstay in previs and digital cinematography since 2003. A comic-book artist turned character animator, he's designed, animated, and photographed some of the most dynamic and memorable sequences from *The Transformers*, *I Am Legend*, and *The Amazing Spider-Man*. Monty has also designed sequences for full CG feature animation at Blue Sky Studios and Curious Pictures. At Proof, he has supervised teams of artists in both exploratory pitch animatics and conventional previs for *Akira*, *42*, *Green Lantern*, *Tropic Thunder*, and *Bedtime Stories*. As an avid reader of Captain America during Mark Waid's run on the character, it was a dream for him to supervise the previs team on *Captain America: The Winter Soldier*. He has a BA in Computer Animation and an AAS in Illustration from The Fashion Institute of Technology in New York.

Animatics Editor **Coral D'Alessandro** has made a name for herself as one of the top animatics editors in the industry. Starting her career as an assistant editor on the *Narnia* series, she played a key role in creating the animatics for *The Chronicles of Narnia: The Voyage of Dawn Treader*. After spending time at an independent animation studio cutting their storyboards, she joined the Marvel family on *Avengers* and has had her hand in crafting the animatics for *Iron Man 3*, *Thor: The Dark World* and the upcoming *Avengers: Age of Ultron*.

Animatic Artist **James Rothwell**, an entertainment-industry veteran for 18 years, has worked on such films as *Mission Impossible 5*, *Goosebumps*, *Monster Trucks*, *Ant-Man*, *Captain America: The Winter Soldier*, *Cowboys & Aliens*, *Thor*, *Iron Man* and *Iron Man 2*, *Spider-Man 2*, *Rise of the Apes*, *Angels & Demons*, *The Hulk*, *Charlotte's Web*, *Faster*, *Outlander*, and many others. James has also produced and edited his own animated version of Orson Welles' *The Hitch-Hiker* which was accepted at the Hollywood Film Festival and the Los Angeles Film Festival and screened all over the U.S., winning at the Rhode Island Film Festival and a finalist at the 34th Annual USA Film Festival.

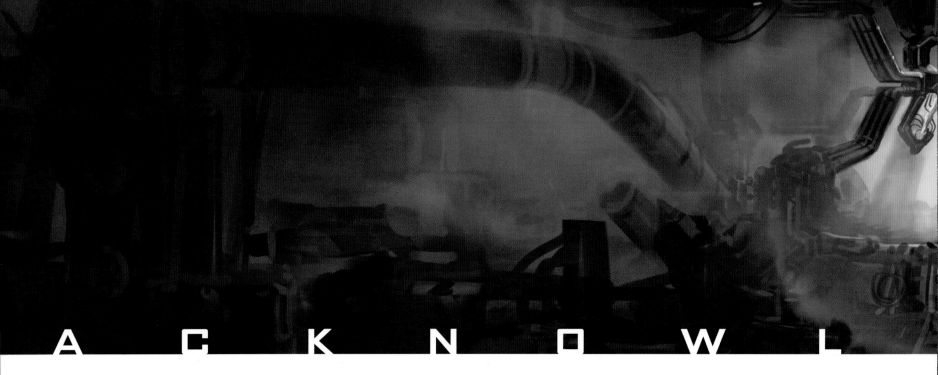

ACKNOWL

Victoria Alonso

Richard Bennett

Russell Bobbitt

Ed Brubaker

James Carson

Stefano Caselli

Kenneth Choi

Tomm Coker

Christian Cordella

Coral D'Alessandro

Federico D'Alessandro

Frank D'Armata

Dan DeLeeuw

Darrin Denlinger

Kim DeMulder

Louis D'Esposito

Mariano Diaz

Dale Eaglesham

John Eaves

Steve Epting

Chris Evans

Kevin Feige

JJ Field

Tim Flattery

Daniel Freedman

Rodney Fuentebella

Sunny Gho

Monty Granito

Frank Grillo

Michael Grillo

Bryan Hitch

Samuel L. Jackson

Bernie Jaye

Scarlett Johansson

Jacob Johnston

Andrew Kim

ACKNOWLEDGMENTS

Theodore W. Kutt
Stan Lee
Derek Luke
Anthony Mackie
Shane Mahan
Judianna Makovsky
Laura Martin
Neal McDonough
Steve McFeely

Rob McKinnon
Ryan Meinerding
Nate Moore
David Moreau
Paul Neary
Josh Nizzi
Trent Opaloch
Andy Park
Julien Pougnier

Anshuman Prasad
Jamie Rama
Robert Redford
Bruno Ricci
Christopher Ross
Luke Ross
James Rothwell
Anthony & Joe Russo
Sebastian Stan

Georges St-Pierre
Chris Swift
Trinh Tran
Andy Troy
Jen Underdahl
Peter Wenham

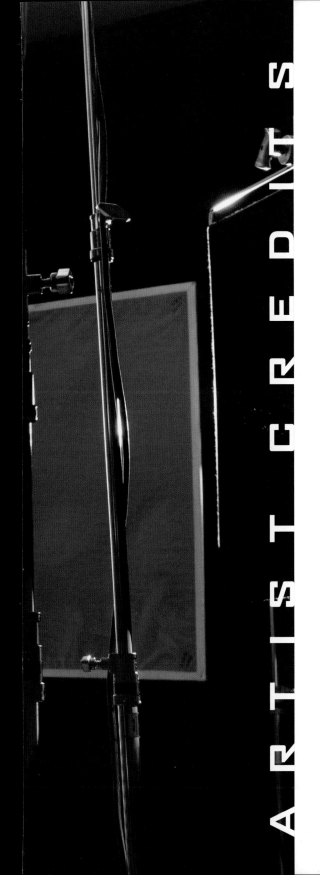

ARTIST CREDITS

Ryan Meinerding
Pages 2-3, 20-21, 46-53, 56-63, 106-111,
142-145, 166-169, 183, 216-218, 222-227,
Cover, Gatefold

Rodney Fuentebella
Pages 4-7, 33, 114-115, 120-123, 140-141,
146-147, 170-171, 174-175, 194-195,
208-214

Andrew Kim
Pages 16-17, 32, 135-137, 206-207

James Carson
Pages 18-19, 64-67, 70-71, 102-105,
112-113

Andy Park
Pages 24-25, 77, 182

John Eaves
Pages 28-29, 95

Christian Cordella
Pages 30, 92, 154-155

Mariano Diaz
Page 32

Darrin Denlinger
Pages 36-43, 88-89, 96-97, 134,
138-139, 156-163, 200-205

David Moreau
Pages 54-55, 64-67; 90-91

Jamie Rama
Pages 74-83, 88-89, 128-133

Tim Flattery
Pages 84-85, 94

Rob McKinnon
Pages 44-45, 98-99

Industrial Light & Magic
Pages 86-87

Monty Granito
Pages 116-120, 120-121, 124-125, 156-163,
188-189

Josh Nizzi
Pages 148-149, 172-173, 178-181, 186-187

Legacy Effects
Pages 150-151, 184-185

Rico D'Alessandro
Pages 196-199

Carol D'Alessandro
Pages 156-163